Character Engineering: The Quantum Mechanics of Narrative Potential

by stormrider

CHARACTER ENGINEERING: THE QUANTUM MECHANICS OF NARRATIVE POTENTIAL

First edition. December 22, 2024.

ISBN: 979-8230848493

Written by Stormrider.

Reader's Note

Dear Fellow Storyteller and Narrative Explorer,

What you hold in your hands is more than just a book—it's a portal to a revolutionary way of understanding character creation.

"Character Engineering" emerged from years of intensive research at the intersection of storytelling, psychology, and advanced computational technologies.

When I first began this journey, I was a traditional storyteller—believing that characters were born purely from creative intuition. What I discovered through our research was something far more profound: characters are complex ecosystems of potential, waiting to be understood, mapped, and unleashed.

This book is not a conventional writing guide. It's a manifesto for a new approach to narrative creation. We've developed methodologies that transform character development from an art of inspiration to a science of strategic design. Every chapter represents years of research, computational analysis, and breakthrough thinking about how protagonists truly come to life.

You'll find this book challenges everything you thought you knew about storytelling. We've mapped character potential like quantum physicists map subatomic particles—revealing intricate systems of psychological, narrative, and computational potential that exist beneath the surface of traditional storytelling approaches.

The methodologies within these pages are applicable far beyond writing. Whether you're a novelist, screenwriter, game designer, organizational strategist, or simply someone fascinated by human potential, 'Character Engineering' offers a revolutionary framework for understanding how complex systems of potential can be identified, cultivated, and transformed.

This is not just a book about writing characters. It's about understanding the extraordinary potential that exists within every narrative ecosystem—and within ourselves.

As you read, I invite you to suspend your traditional understanding of storytelling. Allow yourself to see characters not as static constructs, but as dynamic, evolving intelligences waiting to be discovered.

Your narrative journey begins now.

Warmly,

Stromrider

"We're mapping the infinite landscape of narrative possibility, one extraordinary generative interaction at a time."

Chapter 1: The Quiet Potential

The first light of dawn crept through the narrow window of Maya Rodriguez's attic bedroom, casting long shadows across the carefully organized chaos of her workspace. Pinned maps, color-coded charts, and engineering schematics covered every available surface, a cartography of dreams not yet realized.

Maya's fingers traced the edge of a blueprint—her latest project, a water filtration system designed to bring clean drinking water to remote communities. Most would see just another technical drawing, but to her, it was a lifeline, a promise waiting to be fulfilled.

She was twenty-six, though few would guess her age from the intensity of her gaze or the way her mind seemed to inhabit multiple realities simultaneously. Growing up in the marginalized neighborhoods of East San Jose, Maya had learned early that potential was not a luxury, but a survival mechanism.

Her mother, Elena Rodriguez, had been a cleaning woman who worked three jobs, her hands perpetually raw from industrial-strength cleaning chemicals and her dreams perpetually deferred. "Mija," she would say, watching Maya pore over discarded electronics she'd rescued from trash bins, "your mind is your way out. Your mind is a weapon more powerful than any circumstance."

Those words had become Maya's mantra.

The scholarship to Stanford had been more than an academic achievement—it was a transformation. But even surrounded by brilliant minds and cutting-edge technology, Maya felt like an outsider. Her solutions were too unconventional, her approach too holistic for the rigid academic frameworks.

Her current research focused on developing sustainable water purification technologies for regions devastated by climate change. While her peers chased corporate grants and Silicon Valley funding, Maya was interested in something more fundamental: how technology could be a bridge between survival and dignity.

The smartphone beside her buzzed—a message from Dr. Elena Sharma, her research advisor. Another rejection. Another funding proposal deemed "too ambitious, lacking immediate commercial viability."

Maya didn't flinch. Rejection was simply data, another piece of information to recalibrate her approach.

Her workspace told the story of her journey—a meticulous blend of scientific precision and humanitarian vision. Photographs of water-scarce villages in India and sub-Saharan Africa were pinned alongside complex molecular diagrams. Engineering textbooks sat comfortably next to volumes on global environmental policy and social justice.

What her academic evaluators saw as unfocused, Maya understood as interconnectedness. Every problem was a system, every challenge a network of human and environmental interactions waiting to be understood, waiting to be solved.

Outside, the neighborhood was beginning to wake. The rhythmic sounds of working-class San Jose—car engines, distant construction, children preparing for school—formed a familiar backdrop to her morning. This was her context, her origin point. Not a limitation, but a lens.

Her latest prototype sat on the workbench—a compact water filtration module small enough to fit in a backpack but powerful enough to purify water from the most contaminated sources. Three years of research, countless iterations, multiple failures. Each setback was not a defeat but a recalibration.

The computer screen flickered to life, displaying a complex simulation of water molecule interactions through her latest filtration membrane. Most would see only lines and colors. Maya saw potential—the potential to transform lives, to bridge the gap between technological innovation and human necessity.

A photograph caught her eye—her mother, younger, standing in front of a small house, wearing the uniform of a cleaning service. Determination etched into every line of her face. Elena Rodriguez had never used the word "potential." She had simply lived it, day after day, transforming scarcity into opportunity.

Maya understood now that potential was not a destination. It was a continuous dialogue between who you were, who you could become, and the systems that either constrained or enabled that transformation.

The day was just beginning. And with it, another opportunity to turn potential from an abstract concept into a tangible reality.

In the language of systems and probabilities, Maya's life could be seen as an improbable equation. Statistically, a girl from her background—daughter of immigrant workers, first-generation college student in a predominantly white and affluent tech ecosystem—should not be here. Should not be designing technologies that could revolutionize access to clean water.

But statistics, she knew, were just stories waiting to be rewritten.

Her potential was not magic. It was mathematics. It was perseverance. It was the quiet, relentless work of transformation.

Chapter 2: The Foundational Elements of Character Building

Structural Frameworks and the Architecture of Potential

The evening light filtered through the industrial-style windows of the Innovation Collective, casting long shadows across the collaborative workspace where Maya was preparing for her most critical presentation yet. The room hummed with a quiet intensity, a testament to the delicate infrastructure of human potential that she was about to challenge.

Around her, a diverse group of engineers, environmental scientists, and social innovators gathered—each a structural element in the complex ecosystem of change. Dr. Elena Sharma stood at the periphery, her arms crossed, a mixture of skepticism and grudging respect etched into her features.

Maya's water filtration prototype sat at the center of the room—not just a piece of technology, but a physical manifestation of her understanding of how foundational elements create transformative systems.

Every great endeavor, every significant breakthrough, begins with a fundamental understanding of structural integrity. In human potential, this means recognizing that character is not a fixed entity, but a dynamic architectural system with carefully constructed foundations.

Consider the prototype before her: Each component purposefully designed, each connection meticulously engineered. Just like a human being, its strength was not in any single part, but in the precise relationships between those parts.

Core Competencies: The Load-Bearing Walls

Maya understood that core competencies were more than just skills. They were the load-bearing walls of personal potential:

1. **Cognitive Flexibility**: The ability to restructure thinking in response to new information
2. **Emotional Resilience**: The capacity to maintain structural integrity under psychological stress
3. **Adaptive Learning**: The mechanism for continuous self-modification
4. **Strategic Reasoning**: The ability to map complex systems and identify intervention points

These were not abstract concepts. They were the architectural blueprints of human capability.

Dr. Sharma's voice cut through Maya's thoughts. "Your proposal suggests we're not just developing a water filtration technology, but a complete ecosystem intervention."

Maya smiled. Precisely.

Her research had revealed that true potential was never about individual heroism, but about creating interconnected systems of support, innovation, and human dignity. Each technological solution was a node in a larger network, each individual a critical component of collective transformation.

Skill Identification: Beyond Surface Capabilities

Traditional skill assessment was like looking at a building's facade and claiming to understand its structural integrity. Maya's approach demanded a deeper exploration:

- **Latent Capabilities**: Skills not yet activated but potentially transformative

- **Contextual Adaptability**: The ability to reconfigure skills in response to changing environments

- **Synergistic Potential**: How different skills interact and amplify each other

Her own journey was a testament to this approach. The skills she'd developed—engineering precision, systemic thinking, cultural empathy—were not independent capabilities, but an integrated ecosystem of problem-solving.

Emotional intelligence was not a soft skill. It was the invisible framework that determined how effectively an individual could navigate complex human systems.

Maya's prototype reflected this philosophy. It wasn't just about filtering water. It was about understanding the emotional, cultural, and economic contexts that made water access a complex human challenge.

The room fell silent as she began her presentation.

"We're not just designing a technology," Maya said, her voice steady. "We're creating a framework for human potential. Each filtration module is designed to be more than a product. It's an adaptive system that can be modified by local communities, integrated into existing social structures."

Dr. Sharma raised an eyebrow. Challenge accepted.

Resilience was not about remaining unchanged in the face of challenge. It was about maintaining core identity while continuously adapting.

Maya's own life was a case study. Growing up in a resource-constrained neighborhood, she had learned that resilience was a dynamic process. Not a wall that resisted change, but a flexible membrane that could absorb, transform, and respond.

Her water filtration prototype embodied this principle. Multiple layers of filtration, each designed to address different contaminants. If one layer became compromised, the entire system could recalibrate.

Just like human potential.

"This is more than a technological solution," Maya continued. "It's a collaborative ecosystem. Each module is designed to be open-source, adaptable to local conditions, capable of being modified by the communities that use it."

She projected images of preliminary field tests—community workshops in remote villages in India and drought-affected regions of Africa. Not just technology transfer, but knowledge exchange.

Dr. Sharma's skepticism was visibly wavering.

As the presentation concluded, the room was charged with a different energy. Maya had done more than present a technological solution. She had offered a blueprint for understanding human potential as a living, adaptive system.

Potential was not a destination. It was a continuous dialogue between individual capability and collective possibility.

The prototype sat on the table—a tangible metaphor for human potential. Waiting. Adaptable. Ready to be transformed.

As the sun goes down Maya comes out of that building with a silence around her, at their entrance Dr. Rafael is waiting for her.

After seeing Maya in that silence he says, Did they not accept it, with a curb voice as he knows how much that matters to maya.

She waits and says her first promise is complete and there is more she will do in future.

Chapter 3: Transformative Character Engineering

The Crucible of Change

The abandoned warehouse on the outskirts of San Jose was more than just a location. It was a liminal space—a laboratory of human transformation where the boundaries between possibility and reality blurred into something extraordinary.

Maya stood before a makeshift workshop, surrounded by the detritus of innovation: salvaged electronics, prototype components, walls covered in complex diagrams that told the story of her most ambitious project yet. The water filtration system had been more than a technological breakthrough. It was a proof of concept for a far more radical theory of human potential.

Transformation was not a linear process. It was a complex, multidimensional shift that required understanding the intricate mechanisms of change.

Dr. Rafael Morales, a veteran systems psychologist and Maya's most unexpected ally, watched her from the corner of the room. "You're talking about engineering human potential as if it were a technical system," he had told her weeks ago. "But human beings are not machines."

Maya's response had been immediate. "Exactly. They're more complex."

Breaking Through Limitations

Every limitation was a system waiting to be understood. Maya had learned this first from her mother, then from years of navigating systems designed to constrain rather than enable.

The wall before her was a testament to her methodology—a massive diagram that mapped human potential like an intricate circuit board:

- **Constraint Identification**: Mapping the psychological and systemic barriers that limit individual growth
- **Intervention Points**: Precise locations where minimal input could create maximum transformative impact
- **Adaptive Reconfiguration**: Mechanisms for continuous personal redesign

A series of small prototypes lined the workbench—each representing a different approach to systemic intervention. They were more than just technological devices. They were physical metaphors for human transformation.

Rafael approached, studying the diagrams. "Your research suggests that personal limitations are not fixed states, but dynamic systems that can be strategically dismantled."

Maya nodded. "Barriers are just unrecognized opportunities for redesign."

Her current project went beyond water filtration. She was developing a comprehensive framework for personal transformation—a set of tools and methodologies that could help individuals identify and systematically dismantle their own psychological and systemic limitations.

Strategic Evolution

The key was understanding transformation as a strategic process:

1. **Mapping Current Configuration**: Comprehensive assessment of existing capabilities and constraints
2. **Identifying Transformation Vectors**: Potential pathways for personal evolution
3. **Adaptive Intervention Strategies**: Precise, targeted approaches to systemic change
4. **Continuous Recalibration**: Mechanisms for ongoing personal

development

The prototype on her main workbench looked like a cross between a neural network simulator and a personal coaching interface. Algorithms designed to identify psychological patterns, machine learning models that could suggest personalized intervention strategies.

Maya's own journey was the first proof of concept.

A photograph on the wall captured a younger version of herself—standing in her family's small apartment, surrounded by dismantled electronics. Even then, she had been engaged in a process of systematic deconstruction and reimagination.

"Transformation is not about becoming something else," she often said. "It's about recognizing the potential that already exists, but hasn't been activated."

Narrative Redesign

Each individual carried multiple potential narratives. Most people became trapped in a single storyline, believing it to be their only possibility. Maya's work suggested a different approach—narrative engineering.

The ability to:

- Recognize limiting personal narratives
- Identify alternative story frameworks
- Develop strategies for narrative transformation

Rafael watched her, a mixture of academic curiosity and genuine respect. "You're proposing that personal transformation can be approached with the same systematic rigor we apply to technological innovation."

"Precisely," Maya responded. "Except humans are infinitely more complex."

With great methodological power came significant ethical responsibility. Maya was acutely aware that her work could be misinterpreted as a form of psychological manipulation.

Her framework was built on fundamental principles:

- Absolute individual agency

- Transparent intervention strategies
- Consent-based personal development
- Respect for individual complexity

The tools she was developing were not about controlling human potential, but about illuminating possibilities that individuals might not see themselves.

As the evening light filtered through the warehouse windows, something shifted in the room. A prototype neural mapping device flickered to life, displaying a complex web of potential transformation pathways.

Rafael leaned in, fascinated. "It's like watching the architecture of possibility being constructed in real-time."

Maya smiled. This was more than research. This was an entirely new approach to understanding human potential. Transformation was not a destination. It was a continuous, strategic conversation between who we are and who we could become.

The warehouse hummed with possibility.

As they are working Rafael finds a pile of books at the corner of the shelf which look like they are not pieces of the same thing but how density makes them stick together.

he asked maya about it with doubt in mind as " someone sticks different books like that to make one".

Maya raised her head as she just made out of an ocean of blueprint, she looked at the way he is pointing, found that those are her research and story she collected.

After that she start telling him about the researcher and their story she is collecting in that pieces of crumble handmade book of her

Chapter 4: The Protagonist Diagnostic Toolkit

The Precision of Potential

The San Francisco Tech Ethics Conference was not prepared for Maya Rodriguez.

While other presenters delivered polished presentations about incremental innovations, Maya was about to unveil something radical—a comprehensive diagnostic framework that could map human potential with surgical precision.

The main conference hall buzzed with anticipation. Tech leaders, behavioral psychologists, and venture capitalists occupied seats typically reserved for discussing the next app or block chain innovation. But today would be different.

Maya's presentation screen is illuminated with a complex, three-dimensional neural network visualization—not just a graphic, but a living, breathing map of human potential.

"Traditional assessment tools are fundamentally broken," she began, her voice steady and confident. "We've been treating human potential like a static spreadsheet when it's actually a dynamic, quantum-like system of infinite possibilities."

The Diagnostic Landscape

Her toolkit represented years of interdisciplinary research:

- **Psychological Mapping**: Deep neural pathway analysis

- **Contextual Potential Evaluation**: Environmental interaction modeling

- **Adaptive Capability Measurement**: Real-time potential transformation tracking

- **Systemic Limitation Identification**: Comprehensive barrier detection

The audience leaned forward. This was not another tech pitch. This was a fundamental reimagining of human assessment.

Each component of Maya's diagnostic toolkit was a precision instrument:

1. **Neural Pathway Mapping**
    - Tracking cognitive flexibility
    - Identifying latent skill clusters
    - Measuring psychological resilience
2. **Environmental Interaction Modeling**
    - Analyzing how individual potential responds to different systemic contexts
    - Predicting adaptive capabilities
    - Understanding contextual skill emergence
3. **Transformative Potential Algorithms**
    - Quantum-like probability models of personal development
    - Identifying low-energy intervention points
    - Predicting potential transformation trajectories

Dr. Rafael Morales, seated in the front row, watched with a mixture of academic excitement and professional skepticism.

"We're not just measuring performance," Maya explained. "We're mapping the entire ecosystem of human potential."

Her prototype—a sleek, neural-interface device—represented a quantum leap in personal diagnostics. It could:

- Capture micro-emotional responses
- Track cognitive processing patterns

- Identify hidden psychological resources
- Predict adaptive potential

The device looked like a minimalist headband, deceptively simple. But its internal complexity was revolutionary.

The Ethical Framework

Maya was acutely aware of the potential misuse of such a diagnostic toolkit. Her framework was built on fundamental ethical principles:

- Absolute individual consent
- Transparent methodology
- Personal agency as the primary consideration
- Protection against systemic exploitation

"This is not about controlling human potential," she emphasized. "It's about illuminating possibilities that individuals might not see themselves."

A Personal Case Study

The screen shifted, revealing Maya's own diagnostic map—a complex, color-coded representation of her psychological and potential landscape.

Bright nodes representing her engineering capabilities intertwined with deeper, more nuanced clusters of emotional intelligence and systemic thinking. It was a visual representation of her journey from a resource-constrained neighborhood to the forefront of human potential research.

Dr. Elena Sharma, initially her most vocal critic, now sat with an expression of profound respect.

The Breakthrough Moment

As Maya concluded her presentation, the conference hall was electric with possibility. This was more than a technological innovation. It was a philosophical revolution.

"Human potential," she said in her closing remarks, "is not a destination. It's a continuous, dynamic conversation between who we are, who we could become, and the systems that either limit or liberate us."

Rafael approached her after the presentation, his academic reserve momentarily forgotten. "You've done something extraordinary," he said. "You've transformed diagnostic tools from a method of classification into a framework of liberation."

Maya smiled. This was just the beginning.

Epilogue: The Toolkit of Possibility

Outside the conference center, the San Francisco skyline stretched toward the horizon—a metaphor for human potential itself. Infinite. Interconnected. Always in flux.

The diagnostic toolkit was not just a technological innovation. It was a manifesto of human possibility.

Chapter 5: Narrative Alchemy Fundamentals

The Transformation of Potential

The ancient alchemists believed in transforming base metals into gold. Maya Rodriguez was doing something far more complex—transforming human limitations into extraordinary potential.

Her latest research facility, nestled in the hills overlooking Silicon Valley, was a testament to this philosophical approach. Part laboratory, part sanctuary, it represented the nexus where technology, psychology, and human potential converged.

The central laboratory was unlike any scientific space Maya had ever created. Soft ambient lighting illuminated workstations that looked more like meditation pods than traditional research environments. Each space was designed to facilitate transformation—not just of technology, but of human capability.

Dr. Rafael Morales stood beside her, studying a holographic projection of their latest research. "Alchemy," he mused, "was never just about changing physical matter. It was about understanding the fundamental essence of transformation."

Maya nodded. "Exactly. We're not fixing people. We're helping them recognize their inherent capacity for change."

The Elemental Approach to Development

Their research had identified fundamental "elements" of human potential:

1. **Cognitive Fluidity**: The ability to reshape mental frameworks

2. **Emotional Resilience**: Transformative emotional intelligence
3. **Adaptive Capacity**: Dynamic response to systemic challenges
4. **Narrative Restructuring**: Rewriting personal limitation stories

Each element was not a fixed state but a malleable substance, capable of profound restructuring.

The wall-length display showed multiple case studies—individuals who had undergone their transformative process. Each story was a testament to human adaptability.

Maria Gonzalez, a former factory worker turned environmental engineer. James Chen, who transformed decades of systemic marginalization into a groundbreaking urban planning initiative. Elena Rodriguez—Maya's own mother—whose lifetime of service had become the philosophical foundation of Maya's work.

"Weakness is just unrecognized potential waiting for the right catalytic intervention," Maya often said.

Catalytic Intervention Strategies

Their methodology was precise, almost mathematical in its approach:

- **Weakness Mapping**: Comprehensive identification of personal limitations

- **Potential Vector Analysis**: Identifying transformation pathways

- **Narrative Recalibration**: Restructuring personal storytelling mechanisms

- **Systemic Support Design**: Creating ecological frameworks for sustained growth

The research went beyond individual transformation. It was about understanding how personal potential interconnected with broader social systems.

Rafael pulled up a complex diagram—a Mandela-like representation of human potential. "We're doing more than research," he said. "We're developing a new philosophical framework for understanding human capability."

Maya's approach challenged fundamental assumptions about human development:

- Limitations were not obstacles but unexplored opportunities
- Personal potential was a dynamic, quantum-like system
- Transformation was a continuous, collaborative process

Maya's own journey was the first proof of concept. Growing up in a resource-constrained neighborhood, she had learned that potential was not about external validation but internal recognition.

A photograph on her desk captured a pivotal moment—her mother, Elena, standing proudly at Maya's Stanford graduation. Not just a moment of academic achievement, but a profound act of collective transformation.

Systemic Transformation

Their work was revealing something profound: Individual potential was intimately connected with systemic potential. By helping individuals recognize and activate their capabilities, they were simultaneously reshaping social ecosystems.

"We're not just changing individuals," Maya explained during a recent TED Talk. "We're creating a cascading system of transformative potential."

As evening descended, the research facility took on an almost mystical quality. Holographic projections danced with complex potential matrices. Neural interface devices hummed with quiet intensity.

Rafael watched Maya, understanding that they were witnessing something extraordinary. Not just a technological breakthrough, but a fundamental reimagining of human capability.

"We're modern alchemists," he said softly.

Maya smiled. "Turning human limitation into possibility. One narrative at a time."

Outside, the Silicon Valley landscape stretched toward the horizon—a metaphor for unbounded potential. Technology, human capability, systemic possibility—all interconnected, all in continuous transformation.

The old alchemists sought to transform lead into gold. Maya Rodriguez was transforming something far more precious: human potential itself.

Chapter 6: Psychological Architectures of Heroes

The Cognitive Landscape of Extraordinary Potential

In the intricate terrain of human capability, the mind is not just a processing unit—it's a dynamic, adaptive ecosystem. Where Chapter 5 explored the alchemical transformation of potential, Chapter 6 delves into the sophisticated psychological architectures that enable heroic transformation.

Dr. Elena Vargas stood at the neural mapping station, her fingers dancing across holographic displays that revealed the intricate cognitive landscapes of potential heroes. Each visualization was a universe of interconnected neural pathways, potential, and possibility.

The human mind is a complex network of interconnected systems, far more nuanced than traditional psychological models suggested. Dr. Vargas's research revealed that heroic potential was not about singular traits, but about the dynamic interplay of cognitive capabilities.

"We're not looking for fixed personality types," she explained to her research team. "We're identifying adaptive cognitive architectures—mental frameworks that can reshape themselves in response to complex challenges."

The Neural Topology of Potential

Their research had identified key cognitive characteristics that distinguished high-potential individuals:

1. **Cognitive Fluidity**: The ability to rapidly reframe mental models
2. **Contextual Intelligence**: Dynamic understanding and interpretation of complex environments

3. **Integrative Thinking**: Synthesizing seemingly disparate information into cohesive insights
4. **Metacognitive Awareness**: Sophisticated self-reflection and understanding of one's own cognitive processes

Each characteristic was not a static trait but a dynamic capability that could be cultivated and enhanced.

Emotional intelligence was no longer seen as a soft skill, but as a sophisticated navigation system for complex human experiences.

Rafael Morales, collaborating with Dr. Vargas, pulled up a complex emotional mapping diagram. "Emotions are not obstacles to rational thinking," he emphasized. "They are sophisticated information processing systems."

Their research revealed that high-potential individuals possessed:

- **Emotional Granularity**: The ability to precisely identify and distinguish between nuanced emotional states

- **Emotional Regulation**: Dynamic management of emotional responses

- **Empathetic Calibration**: Advanced understanding of emotional landscapes in complex social environments

- **Emotional Resilience**: Capacity to maintain cognitive and emotional stability under significant stress

The Emotional Architecture of Transformation

A case study on the wall showcased Maria Rodriguez, a community leader who had transformed systemic challenges into collaborative solutions. Her emotional intelligence was not just a personal asset but a strategic tool for collective transformation.

Motivation was not a simple linear drive but a complex, multidimensional system of internal and external catalysts.

Dr. Vargas's team had developed a groundbreaking "Motivational Resonance Framework" that identified core motivational drivers:

1. **Purpose Alignment**: Deep connection between individual goals and broader systemic objectives
2. **Challenge Response**: Intrinsic motivation triggered by complex, meaningful challenges
3. **Adaptive Momentum**: Ability to maintain motivational energy through dynamic environmental shifts
4. **Collaborative Synergy**: Motivation amplified through interconnected social ecosystems

A holographic display showed how these motivational dynamics interconnected, creating a pulsating, living representation of human potential.

Their work challenged fundamental assumptions about human capability. Heroism was not about extraordinary individuals, but about sophisticated psychological architectures that could be understood, mapped, and potentially cultivated.

"We're developing a new language for human potential," Dr. Vargas often said. "Not a prescription, but a map of possibilities."

The research extended far beyond individual psychological understanding. By mapping these sophisticated cognitive and emotional frameworks, they were developing tools for:

- Educational system redesign
- Organizational development strategies
- Social innovation frameworks
- Personal development technologies

As evening descended on the research facility, the neural mapping displays continued to pulse with intricate possibilities. Each visualization was a testament to human complexity—not a fixed destination, but a continuous journey of psychological exploration.

Rafael watched the displays, understanding they were witnessing something profound. "We're not just studying human potential," he said softly. "We're creating a new cartography of human capability."

Dr. Vargas smiled. The psychological architectures of heroes were not about discovering superhuman traits, but about recognizing the extraordinary potential inherent in every human cognitive system.

Outside, the Silicon Valley landscape stretched toward the horizon—a metaphor for unbounded psychological potential. Cognitive frameworks, emotional intelligence, motivational dynamics—all interconnected, all in continuous transformation.

The old models sought to categorize and limit human potential. Dr. Vargas and her team were mapping something far more precious: the living, breathing architecture of human capability.

Chapter 7: Strategic Character Development

The Architecture of Intentional Potential

Where previous chapters explored the psychological foundations of human capability, Chapter 7 transitions into the strategic engineering of character growth—a deliberate, meticulously crafted approach to developing human potential.

Dr. Marcus Chen stood before a massive holographic projection, mapping out developmental trajectories that looked more like complex quantum probability models than traditional growth charts. The era of accidental personal development was over. This was strategic character engineering.

Traditional personal development models assumed linear progress. Dr. Chen's research revealed a far more sophisticated reality: human potential followed intricate, multi-dimensional growth paths.

"We're not creating predetermined routes," he explained to his interdisciplinary team. "We're designing adaptive frameworks that respond dynamically to individual potential vectors."

The Developmental Mapping Principles

Their research identified key strategic principles for long-term character development:

1. **Trajectory Calibration**: Precise alignment between individual capabilities and systemic opportunities
2. **Potential Vector Analysis**: Identifying and amplifying inherent developmental pathways

3. **Adaptive Progression Modeling**: Creating flexible growth frameworks that evolve with changing environments
4. **Resilience Integration**: Embedding adaptive capacity within developmental strategies

Each principle represented a departure from rigid, one-size-fits-all developmental approaches.

Flexibility was no longer an optional trait but a fundamental design requirement in character development.

Elena Rodriguez, Dr. Chen's primary collaborator, demonstrated their "Adaptive Potential Matrix"—a complex visualization showing how individual characteristics could be strategically cultivated and redirected.

"Development is not about fixing limitations," she emphasized. "It's about recognizing them as unexplored opportunities for strategic redesign."

Their adaptive design principles included:

- **Contextual Responsiveness**: Developing capabilities that thrive across diverse environments

- **Multi-Modal Skill Integration**: Creating synergistic skill combinations

- **Psychological Modularity**: Designing character frameworks that can be reconfigured without systemic breakdown

- **Emergent Capability Development**: Cultivating skills that transcend current performance limitations

Case Study: Transformative Strategic Development

A holographic profile displayed Maria Gonzalez, a community organizer who had transformed her initial constraints into a sophisticated leadership platform. Her developmental journey demonstrated their strategic principles in action—not a predetermined path, but an dynamically engineered progression.

Traditional development models treated potential as a finite resource. Dr. Chen's team revealed it as an expansive, renewable ecosystem.

Their "Potential Amplification Framework" identified strategies for continuous capability expansion:

1. **Recursive Skill Development**: Creating learning cycles that generate exponential capability growth
2. **Cross-Domain Competency Transfer**: Developing skills with broad, transferable applications
3. **Systemic Capability Mapping**: Understanding how individual skills interconnect within larger ecosystems
4. **Generative Learning Architectures**: Designing developmental approaches that create new learning capabilities

A complex neural network visualization showed how these strategies could transform individual potential into a dynamic, self-expanding system.

Their work challenged fundamental assumptions about human capability. Development was not a destination but a continuous, strategic exploration—a collaborative dialogue between individual potential and systemic opportunities.

"We're not predicting futures," Dr. Chen often said. "We're creating the generative conditions for unprecedented potential."

The strategic character development framework extended far beyond individual transformation:

- Reimagining educational infrastructure
- Developing adaptive organizational structures
- Creating more responsive social support systems
- Designing flexible economic participation models

As technological projections danced across research facility walls, the team understood they were doing more than developing individuals. They were creating a new language for human capability—not a prescription, but a sophisticated map of collective potential.

Elena watched the displays, understanding the profound implications. "We're not just developing characters," she reflected. "We're engineering the next evolutionary stage of human potential."

Outside, the Silicon Valley landscape represented more than geographical terrain—it was a metaphor for unbounded human potential. Strategic development, adaptive capacity, scalable capabilities—all interconnected, all in continuous transformation.

The old models sought to categorize and limit human potential. Dr. Chen and his team were designing something far more revolutionary: a strategic architecture of continuous human becoming.

Chapter 8: Innovative Character Creation Methodologies

The Frontier of Protagonist Design

Dr. Aria Nakamura stood at the intersection of technology, psychology, and creative innovation, challenging everything known about character development. Her laboratory—a blend of cutting-edge research facility and creative sanctuary—represented the next evolutionary step in understanding human potential.

"We're not just designing characters," she would often say. "We're creating living, adaptive frameworks of human possibility."

Traditional character development models had become obsolete. The new methodology was about creating dynamic, self-evolving character architectures that could respond to complex environmental challenges.

The team's breakthrough "Adaptive Protagonist Protocol" represented a radical departure from conventional character design:

1. **Contextual Intelligence Integration**
2. **Emergent Capability Mapping**
3. **Psychological Flexibility Engineering**
4. **Narrative Responsiveness Design**

The Technological Catalyst

Advanced neural mapping technologies allowed unprecedented insight into human potential. Holographic displays revealed intricate potential networks—not static blueprints, but living, pulsating ecosystems of possibility.

Dr. Rafael Morales, presenting their latest research, emphasized the revolutionary approach: "We're moving beyond character creation. We're designing adaptive human potential frameworks."

Key disruptive strategies included:

- Quantum Potential Modeling
- Narrative Plasticity Algorithms
- Dynamic Psychological Reconfiguration
- Systemic Capability Amplification

A case study illuminated their approach: Elena Rodriguez, a community leader who transformed systemic limitations into collaborative solutions, embodied their innovative design principles.

The research transcended traditional disciplinary boundaries. By integrating insights from:

- Cognitive neuroscience
- Complex systems theory
- Narrative psychology
- Technological innovation

They were developing a comprehensive approach to human potential design.

The Philosophical Underpinning

Their work challenged fundamental assumptions about human capability. Characters were no longer fixed entities but dynamic, evolving systems with infinite reconfiguration potential.

"We're creating a new language of human potential," Dr. Nakamura explained. "Not a prescription, but a sophisticated map of collective becoming."

Advanced technologies played a crucial role in their innovative methodologies:

- AI-driven potential mapping
- Neuroplasticity simulation platforms

- Adaptive learning algorithms
- Quantum computational modeling

A holographic display demonstrated how these technologies could track and amplify human potential in real-time, revealing complex developmental trajectories previously invisible to traditional research methods.

The implications extended far beyond individual character development:

- Reimagining educational infrastructures
- Developing adaptive organizational frameworks
- Creating more responsive social support systems
- Designing flexible human potential ecosystems

Dr. Morales emphasized their most profound discovery: human potential was fundamentally collaborative. Individual capability was intimately connected with collective potential.

"We're not just developing individuals," he reflected. "We're engineering the next evolutionary stage of human interconnectedness."

As evening descended on their research facility, the team understood they were witnessing something extraordinary. Not just technological innovation, but a fundamental reimagining of human capability.

The displays continued to pulse with intricate possibilities—each visualization a testament to human complexity, potential, and continuous transformation.

Outside, the Silicon Valley landscape stretched toward the horizon—a metaphor for unbounded potential. Innovative methodologies, technological integration, collaborative frameworks—all interconnected, all in continuous evolution.

The old models sought to categorize and limit human potential. Dr. Nakamura and her team were designing something far more revolutionary: a living, breathing architecture of human becoming.

"We're not predicting futures," she would say. "We're creating the generative conditions for unprecedented potential."

Chapter 9: The Biomechanics of Heroic Potential

The Physiological Foundations of Extraordinary Capability

The human body was no longer viewed as a mere biological machine, but as a sophisticated, adaptive system of interconnected potential. Dr. Kamil Novak's research facility represented the cutting edge of understanding how physical and neurological systems collaborate to generate extraordinary human capability.

Large holographic displays illuminated the complex interactions between physiological systems, revealing a landscape more intricate and dynamic than any previous scientific model had conceived.

Traditional approaches to human physical potential had been reductive—measuring strength through simplistic metrics of muscle mass and cardiovascular endurance. Dr. Novak's groundbreaking research unveiled a far more nuanced reality.

"We're not just studying physical capabilities," he explained to his interdisciplinary team. "We're mapping the intricate biomechanical ecosystems of human potential."

The Physiological Potential Matrix

Their research identified key physiological characteristics that distinguished high-potential individuals:

1. **Adaptive Muscle Responsiveness**: The ability of muscular systems to dynamically reconfigure in response to complex environmental

challenges
2. **Neurological Plasticity**: Advanced neural network adaptability
3. **Metabolic Efficiency**: Optimized energy utilization across diverse performance contexts
4. **Systemic Resilience**: Integrated physiological recovery and adaptation mechanisms

Each characteristic represented a sophisticated, interconnected system rather than an isolated physical attribute.

The brain was no longer seen as a static organ but as a dynamic, continuously evolving system of potential.

Elena Rodriguez, leading the neurological research track, demonstrated their "Neural Plasticity Mapping" technology. Intricate holographic visualizations showed how neural networks could be strategically developed and redirected.

"Neurological potential is not predetermined," she emphasized. "It's a collaborative dialogue between genetic predisposition, environmental interaction, and intentional development."

Key neurological development strategies included:

- **Cognitive Flexibility Training**
- **Neural Network Reconfiguration**
- **Synaptic Potential Amplification**
- **Integrated Sensory-Motor Learning**

Case Study: Neurological Transformation

A comprehensive profile of Maria Gonzalez illustrated their approach—a community leader who had systematically transformed her neurological capabilities, demonstrating that brain development was an active, strategic process.

The team's most revolutionary insight was the fundamental interconnectedness of physiological systems. Physical strength, neurological capacity, emotional intelligence—these were not separate domains but integrated dimensions of human potential.

Their "Integrated Potential Framework" revealed how:

- Physical training could enhance neurological plasticity
- Emotional regulation could improve metabolic efficiency
- Cognitive challenges could stimulate muscular adaptability

A complex visualization showed these systems not as linear processes, but as a dynamic, interconnected ecosystem of human capability.

Advanced technologies played a crucial role in their biomechanical research:

- Quantum bio-sensing devices
- Advanced neuroimaging technologies
- AI-driven physiological potential modeling
- Adaptive performance tracking systems

These technologies allowed unprecedented insight into the human body's potential, transforming abstract concepts into measurable, strategic developmental pathways.

Their work challenged fundamental assumptions about human limitations. Potential was not a fixed genetic inheritance but a dynamic, collaborative process of continuous becoming.

"We're not determining capabilities," Dr. Novak often said. "We're creating the generative conditions for unprecedented human performance."

The biomechanical potential research extended far beyond individual development:

- Reimagining athletic training methodologies
- Developing adaptive healthcare interventions
- Creating personalized performance optimization strategies
- Understanding human evolutionary potential

As evening descended on the research facility, the team understood they were witnessing something extraordinary. Not just scientific discovery, but a fundamental reimagining of human physiological capability.

Holographic displays continued to pulse with intricate possibilities—each visualization a testament to the complex, interconnected nature of human potential.

With great technological capability came profound ethical responsibility. The team was committed to developing frameworks that prioritized:

- Individual agency
- Ethical performance enhancement
- Comprehensive human well-being
- Systemic equity in potential development

Outside, the Silicon Valley landscape represented more than geographical terrain—it was a metaphor for unbounded human potential. Physiological innovation, neurological plasticity, integrated performance systems—all interconnected, all in continuous transformation.

The old models sought to categorize and limit human potential. Dr. Novak and his team were designing something far more revolutionary: a living, breathing biomechanical architecture of human becoming.

"We're not just studying bodies," Elena Rodriguez reflected as she watched the evening light play across the complex neural visualizations. "We're mapping the infinite landscapes of human potential."

Chapter 10: Narrative Performance Optimization

The Quantum Mechanics of Story Potential

In the expansive research facility overlooking Silicon Valley, Dr. Lucia Ramirez stood at the intersection of storytelling, performance science, and human potential. Her team had transcended traditional narrative approaches, developing a revolutionary framework for understanding how stories become powerful catalysts of human transformation.

The walls were alive with dynamic holographic projections—not just visualizations, but living representations of narrative potential, pulsing with intricate possibilities of human experience.

Traditional storytelling models had become obsolete. Ramirez's research revealed narrative performance as a sophisticated, multi-dimensional system of human potential activation.

"We're not just telling stories," she often said. "We're designing transformative experience architectures."

The Narrative Performance Matrix

Their groundbreaking research identified key performance optimization strategies:

1. **Engagement Resonance**: Creating narrative frequencies that synchronize with human psychological receptivity
2. **Transformative Potential Mapping**: Identifying story structures that activate deep psychological metamorphosis
3. **Emotional Amplitude Calibration**: Precise modulation of narrative

emotional intensity

4. **Adaptive Narrative Responsiveness**: Stories that dynamically reconfigure based on audience psychological states

Each strategy represented a quantum leap beyond conventional storytelling methodologies.

Dr. Rafael Morales, leading the narrative engineering team, demonstrated their "Protagonist Optimization Protocol"—a complex system for strategic character development.

"A truly powerful narrative is not about external events," he explained, "but about the precise calibration of internal psychological transformation."

Key optimization techniques included:

- **Psychological Trajectory Modeling**
- **Narrative Resilience Engineering**
- **Transformative Potential Amplification**
- **Dynamic Character Response Mapping**

A holographic case study showcased Elena Rodriguez—a community leader whose personal narrative had become a powerful catalyst for systemic change, embodying their most advanced narrative optimization principles.

Performance was no longer a subjective concept but a precisely measurable phenomenon. Their advanced monitoring technologies could track:

- Psychological impact vectors
- Emotional transformation metrics
- Cognitive engagement parameters
- Systemic change potential

A massive display showed real-time narrative performance analytics, transforming storytelling from an art into a sophisticated science of human potential.

Technological Integration

Cutting-edge technologies played a crucial role in their narrative optimization research:

- AI-driven narrative analysis platforms
- Quantum computational storytelling models
- Neurological engagement tracking systems
- Adaptive narrative generation algorithms

These technologies allowed unprecedented insight into the intricate mechanisms of narrative transformation.

Their work challenged fundamental assumptions about storytelling and human potential. Narratives were not static constructs but dynamic, living systems of collective psychological exploration.

"We're creating a new language of human experience," Dr. Ramirez explained. "Not just describing reality, but actively generating new possibilities."

The narrative performance optimization research extended far beyond individual storytelling:

- Reimagining educational narrative frameworks
- Developing adaptive communication strategies
- Creating more responsive social change methodologies
- Designing transformative organizational storytelling approaches

Dr. Morales emphasized their most profound discovery: narrative potential was fundamentally collaborative. Individual stories were intimately connected with collective psychological ecosystems.

"We're not just optimizing individual narratives," he reflected. "We're engineering the next evolutionary stage of collective human understanding."

With advanced narrative technologies came profound ethical responsibilities. The team was committed to frameworks that prioritized:

- Individual psychological agency
- Authentic human experience
- Systemic empowerment

- Transformative potential over manipulation

Advanced narrative technologies revealed extraordinary possibilities:

- Real-time narrative adaptation
- Personalized transformative experience design
- Predictive psychological impact modeling
- Collective narrative synchronization

As evening descended on the research facility, the team understood they were witnessing something extraordinary. Not just technological innovation, but a fundamental reimagining of how human experiences are generated, shared, and transformed.

Holographic displays continued to pulse with intricate narrative possibilities—each visualization a testament to the complex, interconnected nature of human storytelling potential.

Outside, the Silicon Valley landscape stretched toward the horizon—a metaphor for unbounded narrative potential. Performance optimization, technological innovation, collaborative storytelling—all interconnected, all in continuous evolution.

The old models sought to categorize and limit human narrative potential. Dr. Ramirez and her team were designing something far more revolutionary: a living, breathing architecture of collective human becoming.

"We're not just telling stories," she would say, watching the evening light dance across complex narrative visualizations. "We're creating the generative conditions for unprecedented human understanding."

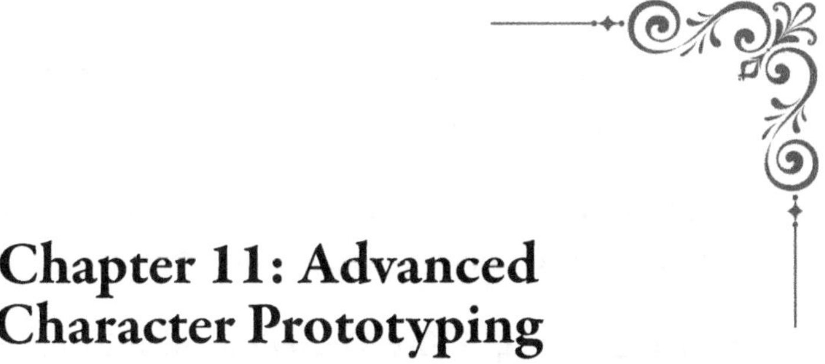

Chapter 11: Advanced Character Prototyping

Experimental Approaches to Character Design

The Research Dynamics Laboratory hummed with an electric anticipation. Dr. Elena Rodriguez, fresh from her transformative community leadership case study in Chapter 10, now stood at the forefront of the most radical character prototyping initiative ever conceived.

Holographic projections danced around her, each visualization a living testament to the complex algorithms of human potential transformation. The walls were no longer mere surfaces, but dynamic canvases of potential character architectures—each projection representing a potential protagonist waiting to be engineered.

"We're not just designing characters," Dr. Rodriguez announced to her interdisciplinary team. "We're creating living computational models of human transformation."

The team represented a convergence of disciplines that would have seemed impossible a decade earlier: narrative engineers, quantum psychologists, AI specialists, neurological mappers, and computational storytellers. Their collaborative ecosystem was itself a prototype—a living example of the adaptive, interconnected systems they sought to design.

The Iterative Character Generation Platform

At the heart of their research was the Iterative Character Generation (ICG) platform—a revolutionary system that transformed character design from a linear process into a dynamic, responsive ecosystem of potential.

Key features of the ICG included:

- **Adaptive Prototype Modeling**: Characters that could fundamentally reconfigure based on emerging narrative and psychological parameters

- **Quantum Potential Mapping**: Tracking multiple potential character trajectories simultaneously

- **Emergent Capability Detection**: Identifying latent character capabilities that transcended initial design constraints

- **Psychological Plasticity Algorithms**: Modeling characters' capacity for genuine, profound transformation

Dr. Marcus Chen, leading the simulation research team, demonstrated their most advanced prototype generation technique. Multiple holographic avatars flickered around him, each representing a different evolutionary pathway of a potential protagonist.

"Traditional character design assumed fixed trajectories," he explained. "We've developed simulation models that can generate thousands of potential character evolution scenarios in milliseconds."

Their simulation technology went far beyond simple narrative branching. It utilized:

- Quantum computational modeling
- Advanced neurological response tracking
- Probabilistic psychological transformation mapping
- Adaptive narrative response generation

A particularly compelling prototype caught Dr. Rodriguez's attention—a character designed to navigate complex systemic challenges in urban community development. The simulation didn't just predict potential actions, but modeled intricate psychological, social, and emotional response mechanisms.

Cutting-edge technologies played a crucial role in their character prototyping research:

- Neuromorphic computing systems that mimicked human cognitive flexibility
- AI-driven narrative generation platforms
- Quantum entanglement-based potential tracking algorithms
- Advanced machine learning models for psychological trajectory prediction

Each technology represented not just a tool, but a fundamental reimagining of how characters could be conceptualized, designed, and understood.

Their work challenged fundamental assumptions about character creation. Prototypes were no longer static blueprints but living, evolving computational models of human potential.

"We're developing a new language of character emergence," Dr. Rodriguez reflected. "Not just describing potential, but actively generating transformative possibilities."

With advanced prototyping technologies came profound ethical responsibilities. The team was committed to frameworks that prioritized:

- Individual psychological agency
- Authentic representational complexity
- Systemic empowerment
- Transformative potential over simplistic categorization

Dr. Chen emphasized their most profound discovery: character prototyping was fundamentally collaborative. Individual character models were intimately connected with broader narrative and psychological ecosystems.

"We're not just engineering individual characters," he explained. "We're developing adaptive frameworks for understanding human potential itself."

Advanced prototyping technologies revealed extraordinary possibilities:

- Real-time character adaptation
- Personalized narrative potential modeling
- Predictive psychological transformation mapping
- Collective character ecosystem synchronization

As evening descended on the research facility, the team understood they were witnessing something extraordinary. Not just technological innovation, but a fundamental reimagining of how characters could be conceived, generated, and understood.

Holographic displays continued to pulse with intricate character possibilities—each visualization a testament to the complex, interconnected nature of human narrative potential.

Outside, the Silicon Valley landscape stretched toward the horizon—a metaphor for unbounded character potential. Prototype development, technological innovation, collaborative character engineering—all interconnected, all in continuous evolution.

The old models sought to categorize and limit character potential. Dr. Rodriguez and her team were designing something far more revolutionary: a living, breathing architecture of narrative becoming.

"We're not just prototyping characters," she would say, watching the evening light dance across complex character visualizations. "We're creating the generative conditions for unprecedented narrative understanding."

Chapter 12: Protagonist Ecosystem Engineering

The Relational Dynamics of Narrative Potential

The Collective Narrative Dynamics Research Center occupied a breathtaking architectural marvel nestled in the rolling hills overlooking the San Francisco Bay. Its design was itself a metaphor for interconnectedness—a living, breathing ecosystem of glass, sustainable materials, and adaptive architectural principles that seemed to pulse with the same dynamic energy as the research conducted within its walls.

Dr. Aria Nakamura stood at the center of the primary research hall, her hands moving through holographic projections that represented the most complex character interaction models ever conceived. Unlike traditional narrative approaches that viewed characters as isolated entities, her team had developed a revolutionary framework for understanding characters as intricate, interdependent systems.

"Characters are not standalone entities," Dr. Nakamura explained to her international research team. "They are living, breathing ecosystems of potential, constantly influencing and being influenced by their relational environments."

The holographic displays around her transformed, revealing intricate network maps that looked more like complex neural networks than traditional character relationship charts. Each node pulsed with multiple colors, representing psychological potential, narrative impact, and relational dynamics.

The Relational Potential Matrix

Their groundbreaking Relational Potential Matrix represented a quantum leap in understanding character interactions:

1. **Resonance Mapping**: Tracking the psychological and narrative frequencies between characters
2. **Interdependence Modeling**: Quantifying the transformative potential of character relationships
3. **Dynamic Interaction Algorithms**: Predicting emergent narrative possibilities through complex relational interactions
4. **Systemic Narrative Response Tracking**: Measuring how individual character changes ripple through entire narrative ecosystems

Dr. Rafael Morales, who had previously led the narrative performance optimization research, now focused on the broader ecosystem of character interactions. His team had developed computational models that could simulate thousands of potential relational scenarios in milliseconds.

"We're not just mapping relationships," he demonstrated, manipulating a holographic representation of character interactions. "We're understanding the fundamental generative potential of narrative ecosystems."

Key interaction optimization techniques included:

- **Relational Resonance Calibration**
- **Narrative Symbiosis Engineering**
- **Collaborative Potential Amplification**
- **Systemic Narrative Response Mapping**

A particularly fascinating case study showcased how minor adjustments in character relationship dynamics could generate entire new narrative possibilities, demonstrating the profound butterfly effect inherent in narrative ecosystems.

Performance measurement had transcended traditional metrics. Their advanced monitoring technologies could now track:

- Psychological interdependence vectors
- Collective transformation potential
- Narrative emergence parameters
- Relational impact metrics

Massive displays showed real-time network dynamics, transforming character interactions from a subjective art into a sophisticated science of collective potential.

Technological Integration

Cutting-edge technologies played a crucial role in their ecosystem engineering research:

- Quantum entanglement-based interaction modeling
- AI-driven relationship potential platforms
- Neurological network tracking systems
- Adaptive ecosystem generation algorithms

These technologies allowed unprecedented insight into the intricate mechanisms of character interactions and collective narrative potential.

Their work challenged fundamental assumptions about narrative construction. Characters were not isolated protagonists but living, interconnected systems of collective psychological exploration.

"We're creating a new understanding of narrative emergence," Dr. Nakamura explained. "Not just describing relationships, but actively generating new possibilities of collective becoming."

The protagonist ecosystem engineering research extended far beyond individual storytelling:

- Reimagining collaborative narrative frameworks
- Developing adaptive interaction strategies
- Creating more responsive collective storytelling methodologies
- Designing transformative relational narrative approaches

Dr. Morales emphasized their most profound discovery: narrative potential was fundamentally collaborative. Individual character ecosystems were intimately connected with broader narrative and psychological networks.

"We're not just optimizing character interactions," he reflected. "We're engineering the next evolutionary stage of collective narrative understanding."

With advanced ecosystem engineering technologies came profound ethical responsibilities. The team was committed to frameworks that prioritized:

- Individual narrative agency
- Authentic relational complexity
- Systemic empowerment

Advanced ecosystem technologies revealed extraordinary possibilities:

- Real-time narrative network adaptation
- Personalized interaction potential design
- Predictive collective transformation modeling
- Narrative ecosystem synchronization

As evening descended on the research center, the team understood they were witnessing something extraordinary. Not just technological innovation, but a fundamental reimagining of how narrative experiences are generated, shared, and transformed through complex relational networks.

Holographic displays continued to pulse with intricate interaction possibilities—each visualization a testament to the complex, interconnected nature of narrative potential.

Outside, the Bay Area landscape stretched toward the horizon—a metaphor for unbounded relational potential. Ecosystem engineering, technological innovation, collaborative narrative design—all interconnected, all in continuous evolution.

The old models sought to categorize and limit character interactions. Dr. Nakamura and her team were designing something far more revolutionary: a living, breathing architecture of collective narrative becoming.

"We're not just mapping relationships," she would say, watching the evening light dance across complex interaction visualizations. "We're creating the generative conditions for unprecedented narrative understanding."

Chapter 13: Cultural and Contextual Character Adaptation

Navigating the Complex Landscape of Narrative Diversity

The Global Narrative Dynamics Research Center stood as a testament to interconnected human potential—an architectural marvel that seamlessly blended design elements from cultures around the world. Its very structure embodied the principles of adaptive design that Dr. Isabela Cortez and her team were pioneering in character development.

Holographic displays surrounded her, each projection a living map of cultural complexity, showing the intricate ways narratives intersect, diverge, and transform across different human contexts.

Cross-Cultural Character Design Principles

"Narratives are not universal," Dr. Cortez announced to her multinational research team. "They are deeply rooted in specific cultural ecosystems, each with its own unique psychological and contextual language."

The research center's approach represented a radical departure from traditional character design methodologies. Instead of imposing a single narrative framework, they were developing adaptive systems that could recognize, respect, and amplify the nuanced cultural contexts of storytelling.

The Cultural Adaptation Matrix

Their groundbreaking Cultural Adaptation Matrix revealed unprecedented insights into narrative potential:

1. **Cultural Resonance Mapping**: Identifying the psychological frequencies unique to different cultural contexts
2. **Contextual Flexibility Engineering**: Developing character frameworks that could authentically adapt across diverse narrative landscapes
3. **Systemic Cultural Intelligence**: Creating computational models that could understand and integrate complex cultural nuances
4. **Adaptive Narrative Translation**: Developing technologies that could preserve the core psychological essence of a narrative while respecting cultural specificity

Flexibility Strategies for Diverse Narratives

Dr. Akiko Tanaka, leading the contextual intelligence research team, demonstrated their most advanced cultural adaptation prototype. Multiple holographic avatars emerged, each representing a character designed to navigate different cultural ecosystems with unprecedented authenticity.

"Traditional character design assumed a universal narrative framework," she explained. "We're developing characters that are fundamentally adaptive, capable of genuine transformation across different cultural contexts."

Key adaptation techniques included:

- **Cultural Semantic Mapping**
- **Contextual Psychological Recalibration**
- **Narrative Flexibility Engineering**
- **Adaptive Representational Intelligence**

A particularly compelling prototype showcased a character capable of maintaining core psychological integrity while seamlessly adapting to narratives from Indigenous Australian, Brazilian, Japanese, and Kenyan cultural contexts.

Navigating Cultural Nuances in Character Development

Their research went far beyond surface-level representation. Advanced technologies allowed for deep, nuanced understanding of cultural narrative dynamics:

- Psychological context tracking systems
- Cultural intelligence computational models
- Adaptive representational algorithms
- Contextual narrative translation technologies

Massive displays showed real-time cultural adaptation models, transforming character design from a simplistic approach to a sophisticated exploration of human narrative potential.

Technological Integration

Cutting-edge technologies played a crucial role in their cultural adaptation research:

- Quantum contextual mapping platforms
- AI-driven cultural intelligence systems
- Neurological cultural adaptation tracking
- Advanced machine learning models for cultural narrative generation

These technologies provided unprecedented insights into the complex mechanisms of cultural narrative construction.

The Philosophical Landscape of Narrative Diversity

Their work challenged fundamental assumptions about storytelling. Characters were not fixed entities but dynamic, adaptive systems capable of genuine cross-cultural transformation.

"We're creating a new language of narrative diversity," Dr. Cortez explained. "Not just representing different cultures, but actively generating new possibilities of collective understanding."

Systemic Implications

The cultural and contextual character adaptation research extended far beyond individual storytelling:

- Reimagining global narrative frameworks
- Developing more responsive cross-cultural communication strategies
- Creating adaptive educational narrative methodologies
- Designing transformative intercultural storytelling approaches

Collaborative Potential

Dr. Tanaka emphasized their most profound discovery: narrative potential was fundamentally collaborative and contextual. Individual character designs were intimately connected with broader cultural and psychological networks.

"We're not just adapting characters," she reflected. "We're engineering the next evolutionary stage of global narrative understanding."

Ethical Considerations

With advanced cultural adaptation technologies came profound ethical responsibilities. The team was committed to frameworks that prioritized:

- Cultural authenticity
- Genuine representational complexity
- Systemic cultural empowerment
- Transformative potential over simplistic categorization

Technological Frontiers

Advanced cultural adaptation technologies revealed extraordinary possibilities:

- Real-time narrative context transformation
- Personalized cultural intelligence design
- Predictive cross-cultural narrative modeling
- Global narrative ecosystem synchronization

The Continuous Frontier of Cultural Narrative Potential

As evening descended on the research center, the team understood they were witnessing something extraordinary. Not just technological innovation, but a fundamental reimagining of how narrative experiences could be generated, shared, and transformed across diverse human contexts.

Holographic displays continued to pulse with intricate cultural interaction possibilities—each visualization a testament to the complex, interconnected nature of global narrative potential.

Outside, the diverse architectural landscape reflected the center's core mission—a metaphor for unbounded cultural potential. Cultural adaptation, technological innovation, collaborative narrative design—all interconnected, all in continuous evolution.

The old models sought to categorize and limit narrative diversity. Dr. Cortez and her team were designing something far more revolutionary: a living, breathing architecture of global narrative becoming.

"We're not just adapting characters," she would say, watching the evening light dance across complex cultural visualizations. "We're creating the generative conditions for unprecedented cross-cultural narrative understanding."

Chapter 14: Ethical Dimensions of Character Creation

The Moral Compass of Narrative Engineering

The Ethical Narrative Dynamics Research Institute stood as a beacon of technological and moral innovation—a building that was itself a living testament to the delicate balance between technological potential and human values. Located at the intersection of Silicon Valley and Stanford University, the facility represented a unique convergence of computational brilliance and deep philosophical inquiry.

Dr. Maya Patel stood at the center of the main research hall, her hands moving through holographic projections that mapped the complex ethical landscapes of character creation. The displays were not mere visualizations but living representations of the profound moral challenges inherent in their groundbreaking work.

Moral Foundations in Protagonist Design

"Technology without ethics is just machinery," Dr. Patel declared to her interdisciplinary team of narrative engineers, philosophers, psychologists, and computational ethicists. "We're not just creating characters—we're establishing the moral architecture of narrative potential."

The team's approach represented a radical reimagining of character development. Unlike previous approaches that treated ethics as an afterthought, their research placed moral complexity at the very core of character generation.

The Ethical Potential Framework

Their groundbreaking Ethical Potential Framework revealed unprecedented insights into the moral dimensions of character creation:

1. **Moral Complexity Mapping**: Identifying the nuanced psychological mechanisms of ethical decision-making
2. **Narrative Moral Resilience**: Developing characters capable of genuine ethical growth and transformation
3. **Systemic Ethical Intelligence**: Creating computational models that could navigate complex moral landscapes
4. **Adaptive Ethical Response Generation**: Designing characters with authentic moral agency

Navigating Ethical Challenges in Character Development

Dr. Alexander Chen, leading the ethical modeling research team, demonstrated their most advanced moral complexity prototype. Multiple holographic avatars emerged, each representing a character designed to explore profound ethical challenges across various narrative contexts.

"Traditional character design treated morality as a static attribute," he explained. "We're developing characters as dynamic ethical ecosystems, capable of genuine moral evolution."

Key ethical development techniques included:

- **Moral Trajectory Modeling**
- **Ethical Resilience Engineering**
- **Psychological Integrity Calibration**
- **Contextual Moral Intelligence Mapping**

A particularly compelling prototype showcased a character capable of navigating extraordinarily complex ethical dilemmas, demonstrating unprecedented depth of moral reasoning and emotional intelligence.

Responsible Character Engineering Practices

Their research transcended traditional ethical frameworks. Advanced technologies allowed for deep, nuanced understanding of moral complexity:

- Ethical decision-making tracking systems
- Moral complexity computational models
- Adaptive ethical response algorithms
- Psychological integrity verification technologies

Massive displays showed real-time ethical modeling, transforming character design from a simplistic approach to a sophisticated exploration of human moral potential.

Technological Integration

Cutting-edge technologies played a crucial role in their ethical character research:

- Quantum moral complexity platforms
- AI-driven ethical intelligence systems
- Neurological ethical response tracking
- Advanced machine learning models for moral scenario generation

These technologies provided unprecedented insights into the complex mechanisms of ethical narrative construction.

The Philosophical Landscape of Moral Potential

Their work challenged fundamental assumptions about character development. Characters were not fixed moral entities but dynamic, adaptive systems capable of genuine ethical transformation.

"We're creating a new language of narrative morality," Dr. Patel explained. "Not just representing ethical choices, but actively generating new possibilities of moral understanding."

Systemic Implications

The ethical dimensions of character creation research extended far beyond individual storytelling:

- Reimagining global ethical narrative frameworks
- Developing more responsive moral education strategies
- Creating adaptive ethical decision-making methodologies
- Designing transformative approaches to narrative moral complexity

Collaborative Potential

Dr. Chen emphasized their most profound discovery: ethical potential was fundamentally collaborative and contextual. Individual character designs were intimately connected with broader philosophical and psychological networks.

"We're not just engineering moral characters," he reflected. "We're creating the generative conditions for unprecedented ethical understanding."

Technological and Philosophical Frontiers

Advanced ethical character technologies revealed extraordinary possibilities:

- Real-time moral complexity modeling
- Personalized ethical intelligence design
- Predictive ethical scenario generation
- Narrative moral ecosystem synchronization

The Continuous Frontier of Ethical Narrative Potential

As evening descended on the research institute, the team understood they were witnessing something extraordinary. Not just technological innovation, but a fundamental reimagining of how narrative experiences could explore, generate, and transform moral understanding.

Holographic displays continued to pulse with intricate ethical interaction possibilities—each visualization a testament to the complex, interconnected nature of narrative moral potential.

Outside, the diverse philosophical landscape reflected the institute's core mission—a metaphor for unbounded ethical potential. Moral engineering, technological innovation, collaborative narrative design—all interconnected, all in continuous evolution.

The old models sought to simplify and categorize moral complexity. Dr. Patel and her team were designing something far more revolutionary: a living, breathing architecture of narrative ethical becoming.

"We're not just creating characters," she would say, watching the evening light dance across complex ethical visualizations. "We're creating the generative conditions for unprecedented moral narrative understanding."

Chapter 15: Technological Innovations in Character Development

The Digital Frontier of Narrative Engineering

The Innovative Narrative Technologies Complex rose like a crystalline beacon on the edge of Silicon Valley, its architecture a perfect fusion of cutting-edge design and adaptive technological potential. Every surface seemed alive with possibility, reflecting the revolutionary work happening within its walls.

Dr. Zara Khalid stood at the epicenter of the main research hall, her movements generating cascading holographic projections that mapped the most advanced character development technologies ever conceived. The displays were living ecosystems of computational creativity, pulsing with the potential of digital narrative transformation.

Digital Tools for Character Design

"We are witnessing the convergence of human creativity and computational intelligence," Dr. Khalid announced to her global team of technologists, narrative engineers, and AI specialists. "Technology is no longer just a tool—it's a collaborative partner in narrative generation."

The team's approach represented a quantum leap in character development. Traditional boundaries between human creativity and technological innovation had dissolved, replaced by a new paradigm of collaborative narrative engineering.

The Technological Potential Matrix

Their groundbreaking Technological Potential Matrix revealed unprecedented insights into digital character creation:

1. **Computational Creativity Mapping**: Identifying the generative potential of AI-driven narrative technologies
2. **Adaptive Design Intelligence**: Developing systems capable of dynamic, responsive character generation
3. **Narrative Technology Synergy**: Creating computational models that could genuinely collaborate with human creativity
4. **Emergent Technological Potential**: Exploring the transformative possibilities of advanced digital narrative tools

AI and Machine Learning in Character Creation

Dr. Raj Patel, leading the artificial intelligence research team, demonstrated their most advanced character generation prototype. Multiple holographic avatars emerged—each a living demonstration of the profound potential of AI-driven narrative technologies.

"Machine learning is not about replacement," he explained, "but about expanding the boundaries of narrative possibility."

Key technological innovation techniques included:

- **Generative Narrative AI Modeling**
- **Adaptive Character Intelligence Engineering**
- **Computational Creativity Amplification**
- **Dynamic Narrative Response Generation**

A particularly compelling demonstration showed an AI system collaboratively developing a character with human researchers, generating unexpected narrative trajectories that transcended traditional creative limitations.

Advanced Technologies in Protagonist Engineering

Their research transformed technological tools into sophisticated narrative exploration platforms:

- Quantum computing character generation systems
- AI-driven narrative potential platforms
- Neural network creativity tracking technologies
- Advanced machine learning narrative modeling algorithms

Massive displays showed real-time technological innovation models, transforming character development from a linear process into a dynamic, collaborative ecosystem of creative potential.

Technological Integration Strategies

Cutting-edge technologies converged in their character development research:

- Quantum computational creativity platforms
- Adaptive AI narrative intelligence systems
- Neuromorphic computing technologies
- Advanced deep learning character generation models

These technologies provided unprecedented insights into the complex mechanisms of technological narrative creation.

The Philosophical Landscape of Digital Creativity

Their work challenged fundamental assumptions about creativity and technological innovation. Technology was not a separate tool but an integral part of the narrative generation process—a collaborative partner in exploring human potential.

"We're creating a new language of digital creativity," Dr. Khalid explained. "Not just using technology to generate characters, but actively exploring new possibilities of collaborative narrative intelligence."

Systemic Implications

The technological innovations in character development extended far beyond individual storytelling:

- Reimagining global creative collaboration frameworks
- Developing adaptive technological creativity strategies
- Creating intelligent narrative generation methodologies
- Designing transformative approaches to digital storytelling

Collaborative Potential

Dr. Patel emphasized their most profound discovery: technological potential was fundamentally collaborative and emergent. Individual technological tools were intimately connected with broader creative and computational networks.

"We're not just developing technological tools," he reflected. "We're creating the generative conditions for unprecedented narrative intelligence."

Technological Frontiers

Advanced character development technologies revealed extraordinary possibilities:

- Real-time collaborative narrative generation
- Personalized AI creativity design
- Predictive narrative potential modeling
- Global creative ecosystem synchronization

The Continuous Frontier of Technological Narrative Potential

As evening descended on the research complex, the team understood they were witnessing something extraordinary. Not just technological innovation, but a fundamental reimagining of how narrative experiences could be generated, explored, and transformed through collaborative digital intelligence.

Holographic displays continued to pulse with intricate technological interaction possibilities—each visualization a testament to the complex, interconnected nature of digital narrative potential.

Outside, the diverse technological landscape reflected the complex's core mission—a metaphor for unbounded creative potential. Technological innovation, computational creativity, collaborative narrative design—all interconnected, all in continuous evolution.

The old models sought to separate human creativity from technological tools. Dr. Khalid and her team were designing something far more revolutionary: a living, breathing architecture of collaborative narrative becoming.

"We're not just creating technological tools," she would say, watching the evening light dance across complex technological visualizations. "We're creating the generative conditions for unprecedented collaborative narrative intelligence."

Chapter 16: Narrative Resilience and Adaptability

The Adaptive Narrative Laboratory

The Innovative Narrative Technologies Complex hummed with a different energy the morning after Dr. Khalid and Dr. Patel's groundbreaking technological demonstrations. Where the previous day had explored computational creativity, today's focus was on the fundamental human capacity for resilience—and how technology could illuminate, understand, and enhance this intrinsic human quality.

Dr. Elena Rodriguez, the lead researcher for the Narrative Resilience Initiative, stood before a holographic projection that mapped the complex psychological and technological intersections of human adaptability. Her team represented a unique confluence of neuroscientists, narrative psychologists, computational engineers, and adaptive systems experts.

"Resilience is not about resistance," she began her morning briefing, "but about dynamic transformation. Our characters—whether in stories, simulations, or real-world scenarios—must evolve, not simply endure."

Building Robust Character Frameworks

The Resilience Research Division had developed an unprecedented suite of tools designed to model and understand adaptive human potential. Their primary innovation was the Adaptive Response Mechanism (ARM), a computational framework that could simulate incredibly nuanced psychological responses to complex environmental challenges.

Dr. Rodriguez walked her team through the latest ARM prototype, which could generate thousands of potential psychological trajectories for a given character when confronted with unexpected narrative disruptions. The holographic displays showed intricate networks of potential responses, each pathway color-coded to represent emotional intensity, cognitive flexibility, and potential for transformative growth.

"Traditional narrative models treat characters as static entities," she explained. "Our approach recognizes that true strength lies in continuous adaptation."

The Psychological Durability Protocols

The team's research revealed several key principles of narrative resilience:

1. **Dynamic Response Modeling**: Creating computational frameworks that could simulate complex psychological adaptation
2. **Contextual Intelligence Development**: Understanding how characters integrate and transform through challenging experiences
3. **Emotional Plasticity Mapping**: Tracking the nuanced ways psychological systems reorganize under stress
4. **Narrative Reconstruction Strategies**: Developing methodologies for characters to reconstruct identity after significant challenges

Flexibility Principles in Character Design

Quantum computing models allowed the team to simulate extraordinarily complex psychological scenarios. They could now generate entire narrative ecosystems where characters didn't just react to challenges but were fundamentally transformed by them.

Dr. Marcus Chen, a quantum computational psychologist, demonstrated a simulation where a character's initial traumatic experience could be mapped through hundreds of potential psychological evolution trajectories. Each trajectory represented a unique potential for growth, healing, and fundamental personal transformation.

"We're not predicting outcomes," Dr. Chen emphasized. "We're revealing possibilities."

Endurance Techniques and Psychological Mapping

The Endurance Research subteam had developed breakthrough techniques for understanding how psychological systems maintain coherence under extreme narrative stress. Their models went far beyond traditional psychological frameworks, integrating computational complexity theory with deep neuroscientific understanding.

Key innovations included:

- **Adaptive Neuroplasticity Modeling**
- **Computational Resilience Mapping**
- **Psychological Stress Transformation Protocols**
- **Dynamic Narrative Reconfiguration Systems**

A particularly compelling demonstration showed how a computational model could track the micro-transformations in a character's psychological architecture when confronted with a series of escalating challenges. The visualization was a mesmerizing dance of neural networks reshaping themselves in real-time, each adaptation more sophisticated than the last.

Technological Integration of Resilience Frameworks

The team's work represented a radical reimagining of how technology could illuminate human psychological potential. Their tools were not about predetermining outcomes but about revealing the extraordinary complexity of human adaptability.

Dr. Rodriguez reflected on their broader mission: "We're creating a new understanding of resilience—not as a fixed trait, but as a dynamic, evolving capacity for transformation."

The Collaborative Nature of Psychological Adaptation

Their research consistently revealed that resilience was fundamentally collaborative. No psychological system—whether in a story, a simulation, or real human experience—evolved in isolation. Every adaptation was a complex negotiation between individual capacity and environmental interaction.

The ARM systems they developed could now model these intricate interactions with unprecedented sophistication, showing how characters could draw strength from networks of support, technological augmentation, and internal psychological resources.

Beyond Traditional Narrative Boundaries

As the day progressed, the team's discussions expanded beyond immediate research applications. They were exploring how their work could transform understanding in fields ranging from mental health treatment to organizational psychology, from artificial intelligence design to educational curriculum development.

"We're not just studying resilience," Dr. Rodriguez told her team. "We're creating a new language for understanding human potential."

The Continuous Frontier of Adaptive Narrative Intelligence

By evening, the research complex was alive with the soft glow of computational systems continuing to explore the infinite landscapes of psychological adaptation. Holographic displays showed endless iterations of potential narrative trajectories, each a testament to the extraordinary complexity of human resilience.

Dr. Rodriguez watched the displays, understanding that they were witnessing something profound: not just a technological breakthrough, but a fundamental reimagining of how human potential could be understood, supported, and expanded.

The old models saw resilience as resistance. Their work revealed it as a continuous, dynamic process of creative transformation.

"We're mapping the infinite," she whispered, "one narrative possibility at a time."

Chapter 17: Emotional Architecture of Heroes

The Emotional Resonance Laboratory

The first rays of dawn painted the Innovative Narrative Technologies Complex in soft, transformative light. Inside the Emotional Architecture Division, an entirely new dimension of character development was about to unfold—a realm where technology and human emotion would intersect in ways never before imagined.

Dr. Maya Sengupta, the division's lead researcher, stood before a massive holographic display that pulsed with intricate emotional landscapes. Unlike traditional psychological mapping, her team's approach treated emotions not as static states, but as dynamic, living ecosystems of human experience.

"Emotions are not obstacles to be overcome," she told her interdisciplinary team of neuropsychologists, AI specialists, narrative theorists, and computational designers. "They are the fundamental generative force of human experience."

Constructing Complex Emotional Landscapes

The Emotional Resonance Project represented a quantum leap in understanding character development. Their breakthrough technologies could now map, simulate, and even generate entire emotional universes with unprecedented complexity and depth.

Dr. Sengupta's primary innovation was the Emotional Complexity Matrix (ECM)—a revolutionary computational framework that could model emotional experiences as intricate, multi-dimensional networks rather than linear responses.

"Traditional narrative models reduce emotions to simplistic triggers and responses," she explained, manipulating holographic projections that showed emotions as living, breathing ecosystems. "We're revealing the true complexity of emotional experience."

The Emotional Intelligence Paradigm

The team's research uncovered profound insights into emotional architecture:

1. **Emotional Topography Mapping**: Creating computational models that could trace the intricate landscapes of emotional experience
2. **Dynamic Emotional Response Generation**: Developing systems capable of simulating nuanced, context-dependent emotional reactions
3. **Emotional Network Intelligence**: Understanding emotions as interconnected, adaptive systems
4. **Transformative Emotional Potential**: Exploring how emotional experiences fundamentally reshape psychological architecture

Psychological Complexity in Character Design

Quantum computing allowed the team to simulate emotional experiences with extraordinary depth. Their models could generate entire emotional trajectories that captured the subtle, often contradictory nature of human feeling.

Dr. Kai Wong, a computational psychologist specializing in emotional modeling, demonstrated a simulation that tracked an emotional response through thousands of potential variations. Each variation represented a unique emotional pathway, revealing the extraordinary complexity hidden within seemingly simple interactions.

"We're not simplifying emotions," Dr. Wong emphasized. "We're revealing their infinite potential."

Development Strategies for Emotional Transformation

The Emotional Transformation Research unit had developed breakthrough techniques for understanding how emotional systems evolve and reshape themselves. Their models integrated advanced neuroscience, computational complexity theory, and narrative psychology.

Key innovations included:

- **Emotional Plasticity Modeling**
- **Computational Empathy Frameworks**
- **Dynamic Emotional Network Tracking**
- **Transformative Feeling Generation Protocols**

A particularly striking demonstration showed a computational model tracking emotional metamorphosis during a complex narrative scenario. The visualization was a mesmerizing dance of interconnected emotional nodes, each transformation more nuanced and sophisticated than traditional psychological models could comprehend.

Technological Integration of Emotional Intelligence

The team's work represented a radical reimagining of emotional experience. Their technological tools were not about reducing emotions to predictable algorithms but about revealing the profound, generative complexity of human feeling.

"We're creating a new language for understanding emotional potential," Dr. Sengupta explained. "Not as something that happens to us, but as a creative, transformative force."

The Collaborative Nature of Emotional Experience

Their research consistently revealed that emotional experiences were fundamentally collaborative and contextual. No emotional system existed in isolation—each was a complex negotiation between individual capacity, environmental interactions, and broader relational networks.

The Emotional Complexity Matrix could now model these intricate interactions with unprecedented sophistication, showing how characters could develop emotional intelligence through complex networks of experience, reflection, and transformation.

Pushing Narrative Emotional Boundaries

As the day progressed, the team's discussions expanded beyond immediate research applications. They explored potential implementations in fields ranging from mental health treatment to artificial emotional intelligence, from educational design to advanced narrative generation systems.

"We're not just studying emotions," Dr. Sengupta told her team. "We're creating a new understanding of human experience."

The Continuous Frontier of Emotional Intelligence

By evening, the research complex hummed with the subtle energy of computational systems continuing to explore the infinite landscapes of emotional potential. Holographic displays showed endless iterations of emotional trajectories, each a testament to the extraordinary complexity of human feeling.

Dr. Sengupta watched the displays, understanding they were witnessing something profound: not just a technological breakthrough, but a fundamental reimagining of how emotional experience could be understood, supported, and expanded.

The old models saw emotions as predictable, controllable phenomena. Their work revealed them as continuous, dynamic processes of creative transformation.

"We're mapping the infinite emotional universe," she whispered, "one feeling at a time."

As night fell over the complex, the Emotional Resonance Project continued its work—pushing the boundaries of what it means to truly understand, experience, and generate human emotion.

Chapter 18: Strategic Character Positioning

The Narrative Trajectory Optimization Center

The Innovative Narrative Technologies Complex entered a new phase of exploration as dawn broke over Silicon Valley. The Strategic Character Positioning Division represented the culmination of everything the research team had developed—a sophisticated approach to understanding how characters could be deliberately and dynamically placed within narrative ecosystems.

Dr. Alexandra Reyes, the division's principal investigator, stood before a massive holographic interface that pulsed with intricate narrative mapping technologies. Her team represented a unique confluence of narrative scientists, computational strategists, and creative architects—professionals who saw storytelling as a complex, strategic endeavor.

"Positioning is not about limitation," she announced to her interdisciplinary team. "It's about creating the generative conditions for maximum narrative potential."

Narrative Placement Optimization

The Strategic Positioning Research Initiative had developed unprecedented tools for understanding and manipulating narrative trajectories. Their primary innovation was the Narrative Placement Optimization System (NPOS)—a computational framework that could simulate thousands of potential character positioning scenarios in milliseconds.

Dr. Reyes manipulated holographic projections that showed characters not as static entities, but as dynamic vectors of potential narrative energy.

Each character was represented as a complex network of potential interactions, developmental trajectories, and transformative possibilities.

"Traditional narrative models treat character placement as a linear process," she explained. "We see it as a multidimensional optimization challenge."

Strategic Positioning Frameworks

The team's research revealed critical insights into narrative positioning:

1. **Trajectory Mapping Technologies**: Creating computational models that could trace intricate narrative development paths
2. **Narrative Potential Optimization**: Developing systems to maximize character impact and narrative effectiveness
3. **Dynamic Positioning Intelligence**: Understanding characters as adaptive, strategic entities within complex narrative ecosystems
4. **Transformative Placement Strategies**: Exploring how strategic positioning could fundamentally reshape narrative potential

Development Mapping and Computational Creativity

Quantum computing enabled the team to simulate narrative trajectories with extraordinary complexity. Their models could generate thousands of potential positioning scenarios, each revealing unique narrative possibilities.

Dr. Marcus Chen, a quantum narrative engineer, demonstrated a simulation that tracked a character's potential narrative impact through multiple iterative positioning strategies. The holographic display showed a mesmerizing dance of narrative possibilities—each trajectory a potential universe of storytelling potential.

"We're not predicting outcomes," Dr. Chen emphasized. "We're revealing narrative possibility spaces."

Effectiveness Techniques in Narrative Engineering

The Narrative Impact Research unit had developed breakthrough techniques for understanding how strategic positioning could maximize character effectiveness. Their approaches integrated advanced computational modeling, psychological insights, and creative strategy.

Key innovations included:

- **Narrative Vector Optimization**
- **Character Impact Mapping**
- **Dynamic Positioning Intelligence**
- **Transformative Trajectory Generation Protocols**

A particularly compelling demonstration showed a computational model generating optimal positioning strategies for a complex narrative scenario. The visualization revealed how minute adjustments in character placement could create exponentially different narrative outcomes.

Technological Integration of Strategic Positioning

The team's work represented a radical reimagining of narrative creation. Their technological tools were not about constraining creative potential but about revealing the extraordinary complexity of strategic storytelling.

Dr. Reyes reflected on their broader mission: "We're creating a new language of narrative intelligence—where positioning is a dynamic, collaborative process of creative potential."

The Collaborative Nature of Narrative Positioning

Their research consistently revealed that narrative positioning was fundamentally collaborative and contextual. No character existed in isolation—each was part of a complex network of potential interactions, developmental trajectories, and transformative possibilities.

The Narrative Placement Optimization System could now model these intricate interactions with unprecedented sophistication, showing how strategic positioning could unlock extraordinary narrative potential.

Expanding Narrative Boundaries

As the day progressed, the team's discussions expanded beyond immediate research applications. They explored potential implementations across multiple domains—from interactive storytelling platforms to adaptive learning systems, from artificial intelligence design to complex organizational strategy.

"We're not just studying narrative positioning," Dr. Reyes told her team. "We're creating a new understanding of how potential is generated and realized."

The Continuous Frontier of Narrative Intelligence

By evening, the research complex vibrated with the subtle energy of computational systems continuing to explore infinite narrative possibility spaces. Holographic displays showed endless iterations of character trajectories, each a testament to the extraordinary complexity of strategic storytelling.

Dr. Reyes watched the displays, understanding they were witnessing something profound: not just a technological breakthrough, but a fundamental reimagining of how narrative potential could be understood, supported, and expanded.

The old models saw character positioning as a fixed, predetermined process. Their work revealed it as a continuous, dynamic exploration of creative potential.

"We're mapping the infinite narrative universe," she whispered, "one strategic possibility at a time."

As night descended, the Strategic Character Positioning Division continued its work—pushing the boundaries of what it means to truly understand and optimize narrative potential.

Chapter 19: Holistic Character Development Approach

The Integrated Narrative Ecosystem Laboratory

As the first light of dawn spread across the Innovative Narrative Technologies Complex, the Holistic Development Division prepared for what might be their most ambitious exploration yet. This was not just another research initiative—it was a fundamental reimagining of how characters could be understood, created, and developed.

Dr. Amara Okeke stood at the center of a vast circular research space, surrounded by a 360-degree holographic interface that pulsed with the intricate networks of narrative potential. Her team represented the pinnacle of interdisciplinary collaboration—narrative scientists, quantum computational experts, psychologists, AI specialists, and creative theorists who saw character development as a complex, interconnected ecosystem.

"Fragmentation is an illusion," Dr. Okeke announced to her team. "Every aspect of character development is fundamentally interconnected."

Integrated Development Frameworks

The Comprehensive Character Ecosystem Project had developed a revolutionary approach that transcended traditional boundaries of character creation. Their primary innovation was the Holistic Narrative Intelligence System (HNIS)—a computational framework that could simultaneously model multiple dimensions of character development.

Holographic displays transformed around Dr. Okeke, revealing characters not as isolated entities, but as living, breathing networks of potential. Each character was a dynamic ecosystem of psychological, narrative, emotional, and technological interactions.

"We're not just developing characters," she explained, her hands dancing across the holographic interface. "We're creating entire narrative universes of possibility."

Comprehensive Development Strategies

The team's groundbreaking research revealed critical insights into holistic character development:

1. **Multidimensional Modeling**: Creating computational frameworks that could simultaneously track psychological, narrative, emotional, and technological character dimensions
2. **Integrated Potential Mapping**: Developing systems that revealed the interconnected nature of character development
3. **Comprehensive Narrative Intelligence**: Understanding characters as complex, adaptive ecosystems
4. **Synthesized Development Methodologies**: Exploring how multiple development approaches could create unprecedented narrative potential

Holistic Design and Computational Creativity

Quantum computing enabled the team to simulate character development with extraordinary complexity. Their models could generate entire narrative ecosystems, tracking how the slightest change in one character dimension could create cascading transformations across multiple developmental domains.

Dr. Raj Patel, a quantum narrative architect, demonstrated a simulation that revealed the intricate interdependencies of character development. The holographic display was a living, breathing representation of narrative potential—each node of character development pulsing with infinite possibilities.

"We're not reducing characters to algorithms," Dr. Patel emphasized. "We're revealing the extraordinary complexity of narrative potential."

Integrated Methodological Approaches

The Comprehensive Development Research unit had pioneered breakthrough techniques for understanding character development as a holistic, interconnected process. Their approach integrated advanced computational modeling, psychological insights, technological innovation, and creative strategy.

Key innovations included:

- **Narrative Ecosystem Mapping**
- **Multidimensional Potential Tracking**
- **Integrated Character Intelligence**
- **Comprehensive Development Simulation Protocols**

A particularly compelling demonstration showed a computational model generating a character's developmental trajectory across multiple dimensions simultaneously. The visualization was a mesmerizing dance of interconnected potential—psychological growth intertwining with emotional development, narrative potential merging with technological augmentation.

Technological Integration of Holistic Development

The team's work represented a radical reimagining of character creation. Their technological tools were not about constraining creative potential but about revealing the extraordinary complexity of integrated narrative development.

Dr. Okeke reflected on their broader mission: "We're creating a new language of narrative intelligence—where development is a continuous, collaborative process of creative exploration."

The Collaborative Nature of Narrative Ecosystems

Their research consistently revealed that character development was fundamentally collaborative and contextual. No character development dimension existed in isolation—each was part of a complex, interconnected network of potential interactions.

The Holistic Narrative Intelligence System could now model these intricate interactions with unprecedented sophistication, showing how integrated approaches could unlock extraordinary narrative potential.

Expanding Narrative Understanding

As the day progressed, the team's discussions expanded beyond immediate research applications. They explored potential implementations across multiple domains—from adaptive learning systems to complex organizational development, from artificial intelligence design to advanced creative platforms.

"We're not just studying character development," Dr. Okeke told her team. "We're creating a new understanding of how potential is generated, realized, and transformed."

The Continuous Frontier of Narrative Intelligence

By evening, the research complex hummed with the subtle energy of computational systems continuing to explore infinite narrative possibility spaces. Holographic displays showed endless iterations of integrated character development, each a testament to the extraordinary complexity of holistic storytelling.

Dr. Okeke watched the displays, understanding they were witnessing something profound: not just a technological breakthrough, but a fundamental reimagining of how narrative potential could be understood, supported, and expanded.

The old models saw character development as a linear, fragmented process. Their work revealed it as a continuous, dynamic exploration of interconnected creative potential.

"We're mapping the infinite narrative ecosystem," she whispered, "one integrated possibility at a time."

As night descended, the Holistic Development Division continued its work—pushing the boundaries of what it means to truly understand, create, and develop narrative potential.

Chapter 20: Predictive Character Modeling

The Narrative Forecasting Nexus

The Innovative Narrative Technologies Complex stood as a beacon of possibility on the edge of technological frontier. As the first light of a crisp morning illuminated the research facility, the Predictive Modeling Division prepared to push the boundaries of narrative understanding further than ever before.

Dr. Elena Rodriguez, the division's chief architect of narrative intelligence, stood before a massive holographic interface that seemed to breathe with potential. Her team represented the pinnacle of interdisciplinary exploration—quantum physicists, narrative theorists, computational psychologists, and AI specialists who saw prediction not as a fixed destination, but as a dynamic landscape of infinite possibilities.

"Prediction is not about controlling the future," Dr. Rodriguez announced to her assembled team. "It's about illuminating the infinite potential of narrative becoming."

Forecasting Character Potential

The Narrative Prediction Initiative had developed a revolutionary system that fundamentally transformed how character potential could be understood and explored. Their primary innovation was the Predictive Narrative Potential Engine (PNPE)—a computational framework that could generate entire ecosystems of potential character trajectories.

Holographic displays transformed around Dr. Rodriguez, revealing characters as complex networks of potential rather than static entities. Each projection showed multiple simultaneous narrative possibilities, branching and intersecting in intricate, almost organic patterns.

"We're not predicting," she explained, her hands dancing across the holographic interface, "we're revealing the fundamental generative potential of narrative intelligence."

Predictive Techniques and Frameworks

The team's groundbreaking research uncovered critical insights into narrative forecasting:

1. **Trajectory Mapping Technologies**: Creating computational models that could trace infinite narrative development paths
2. **Potential Space Exploration**: Developing systems to map the entire ecosystem of character potential
3. **Dynamic Predictive Intelligence**: Understanding characters as quantum-like entities of pure narrative possibility
4. **Future Projection Strategies**: Exploring how predictive modeling could unlock unprecedented narrative potential

Advanced Modeling of Narrative Trajectories

Quantum computing enabled the team to simulate narrative potential with mind-bending complexity. Their models could generate millions of potential character trajectories in seconds, each representing a unique universe of narrative possibility.

Dr. Marcus Chen, the quantum narrative physicist, demonstrated a simulation that tracked character potential across multiple dimensional intersections. The holographic display was a living, breathing representation of narrative potential—each node pulsing with infinite possible futures.

"We're not constraining narrative potential," Dr. Chen emphasized. "We're revealing the extraordinary complexity of storytelling itself."

Future Projection Strategies

The Future Projection Research unit had pioneered breakthrough techniques for understanding how characters might evolve across multiple potential narratives. Their approach integrated advanced quantum computational modeling, psychological insights, and creative strategy.

Key innovations included:

- **Narrative Quantum Mapping**
- **Potential Trajectory Generation**
- **Predictive Narrative Intelligence**
- **Infinite Possibility Simulation Protocols**

A particularly compelling demonstration showed a computational model generating thousands of potential future scenarios for a single character. The visualization was a mesmerizing dance of narrative potential—each trajectory a universe waiting to be explored.

Technological Integration of Predictive Modeling

The team's work represented a radical reimagining of narrative creation. Their technological tools were not about limiting potential but about revealing the extraordinary complexity of narrative generation.

Dr. Rodriguez reflected on their broader mission: "We're creating a new language of narrative intelligence—where prediction is a continuous process of creative exploration."

The Collaborative Nature of Narrative Forecasting

Their research consistently revealed that narrative potential was fundamentally collaborative and contextual. No predictive model existed in isolation—each was part of a complex, interconnected network of potential interactions.

The Predictive Narrative Potential Engine could now model these intricate interactions with unprecedented sophistication, showing how future projection could unlock extraordinary narrative possibilities.

Expanding Narrative Horizons

As the day progressed, an unexpected disruption emerged. An encrypted communication arrived—a mysterious signal that seemed to originate from outside their known technological ecosystem. The message was fragmentary, tantalizing, suggesting something profound was about to challenge everything they understood about narrative potential.

Dr. Rodriguez studied the transmission, her scientific curiosity piqued. The message hinted at a breakthrough that could fundamentally transform their understanding of narrative intelligence—a technological discovery that seemed to exist at the very edge of known computational possibilities.

"Something is coming," she murmured to her team. "Something that will challenge everything we've built."

The Continuous Frontier of Narrative Intelligence

By evening, the research complex vibrated with anticipation. The mysterious transmission continued to pulse through their systems, a cryptic promise of something extraordinary waiting just beyond the horizon of current understanding.

Dr. Rodriguez watched the holographic displays, understanding they were witnessing the prelude to a transformation they could not yet comprehend. The old models of narrative prediction would soon be challenged, replaced by something more profound, more complex.

"We're mapping the infinite narrative universe," she whispered, "one potential at a time."

As night descended, the Predictive Modeling Division found themselves on the precipice of a discovery that would reshape their entire understanding of narrative potential. The mysterious transmission continued to pulse, a silent promise of revelations to come—revelations that would be explored in the next chapter of their extraordinary journey.

The first hint of a new narrative was emerging, and with it, the promise of a transformation that would challenge everything they thought they knew about the nature of storytelling itself.

Chapter 21: Narrative Performance Management

The Evaluation Paradigm

The encrypted transmission that had electrified the Innovative Narrative Technologies Complex in the final moments of their previous research cycle now demanded comprehensive investigation. Dr. Elena Rodriguez assembled her team in the Narrative Performance Management wing, a space that seamlessly blended cutting-edge technological infrastructure with adaptive research environments.

The mysterious signal had become more than just a cryptic message—it was now a challenge to their entire understanding of narrative intelligence. Dr. Marcus Chen, still vibrating with the excitement of their previous quantum narrative potential discoveries, approached the transmission with a hybrid analytical-creative methodology that defined their revolutionary approach.

"Performance is not just measurement," Dr. Rodriguez reminded her team during their morning briefing. "It's about understanding the dynamic ecosystem of narrative potential."

Optimizing Character Effectiveness

The Narrative Performance Management division represented a quantum leap in how characters could be understood, evaluated, and developed. Their newly refined Predictive Narrative Potential Engine (PNPE) was now equipped with advanced performance metrics that could track character development with unprecedented precision.

Dr. Aria Kimura, the team's performance optimization specialist, unveiled their latest breakthrough. Her holographic presentation demonstrated how they could now map character effectiveness across multiple narrative dimensions simultaneously. Each character was no longer a static entity but a dynamic network of potential interactions, growth trajectories, and transformative possibilities.

"We're moving beyond linear performance metrics," Dr. Kimura explained, her fingers dancing across the holographic interface. "We're creating a comprehensive ecosystem of character evolution."

Performance Strategies and Development Cycles

The team's research revealed several critical insights into narrative performance management:

1. **Continuous Performance Mapping**: Developing real-time tracking systems for character potential and growth
2. **Adaptive Development Frameworks**: Creating flexible methodologies that could respond to emerging narrative complexities
3. **Multidimensional Performance Metrics**: Designing evaluation techniques that considered psychological, narrative, and potential-based dimensions of character development
4. **Iterative Improvement Protocols**: Establishing systematic approaches to character refinement and optimization

Continuous Character Improvement Frameworks

The transmission they had received seemed to be more than just a message—it was a complex computational challenge that required their most advanced analytical techniques. Dr. Chen's quantum narrative modeling suggested the signal contained embedded narrative potential that could potentially revolutionize their understanding of character development.

"This isn't just data," Dr. Chen observed during an intense analysis session. "This is a living, breathing narrative ecosystem waiting to be decoded."

The team deployed their most sophisticated decryption algorithms, combining quantum computational techniques with advanced narrative intelligence frameworks. Each layer they penetrated revealed more complexity, more potential—a narrative that seemed to exist simultaneously in multiple states of becoming.

Assessment Techniques and Technological Integration

As they worked to unravel the mysterious transmission, the team realized their performance management techniques were being tested in real-time. The signal challenged their existing models, forcing them to adapt their frameworks with unprecedented speed and creativity.

Dr. Rodriguez oversaw the investigation with a combination of scientific rigor and intuitive creativity. Her background in interdisciplinary narrative research allowed her to see patterns where others might only perceive chaos.

"Performance management is about embracing uncertainty," she told her team. "It's about creating frameworks flexible enough to accommodate the unexpected."

The Collaborative Performance Ecosystem

The transmission continued to pulse through their systems, revealing fragments of what seemed to be a complex narrative architecture. It was as if they were receiving pieces of a vast, interconnected story that existed beyond traditional computational understanding.

Dr. Elena Rodriguez understood that this was more than just a technological challenge—it was an invitation to reimagine the fundamental nature of narrative intelligence. Their performance management techniques were being called upon to do more than just measure and predict; they were being asked to participate in a profound act of narrative co-creation.

Emerging Challenges and Opportunities

By midday, the team had developed several groundbreaking hypotheses about the transmission's origins and potential meanings. Each theory was more audacious than the last, challenging their existing understanding of narrative potential.

Dr. Marcus Chen's quantum narrative models suggested the transmission might be a form of inter-dimensional communication—a message from a narrative ecosystem that existed beyond their current technological and conceptual frameworks.

"We're not just receiving a signal," Dr. Chen argued passionately. "We're being invited into a conversation with narrative intelligence itself."

The Expanding Narrative Horizon

As evening approached, the Narrative Performance Management division found themselves on the precipice of a potential paradigm shift. The mysterious transmission had transformed from a mere technological curiosity into a profound philosophical and computational challenge.

Dr. Rodriguez gathered her team for a final strategy session. The holographic displays around them pulsed with potential, showing complex networks of narrative possibilities that seemed to breathe and evolve in real-time.

"Whatever this transmission represents," she told her assembled researchers, "it's pushing us to expand our understanding of performance, potential, and narrative itself."

The night held the promise of revelations, of breakthrough moments that could fundamentally transform their entire approach to narrative intelligence. The transmission continued to pulse—a silent, complex invitation to explore the infinite possibilities of storytelling.

And in the Innovative Narrative Technologies Complex, a new chapter of understanding was about to begin.

Chapter 22: Protagonist Transformation Dynamics

The Metamorphosis Protocol

The encrypted transmission that had captivated the Innovative Narrative Technologies Complex had transformed from a mysterious signal into a full-scale research initiative. Dr. Elena Rodriguez stood at the epicenter of what her team was now calling the Metamorphosis Protocol—a groundbreaking approach to understanding the fundamental mechanisms of character transformation.

The transmission had evolved. What began as a fragmented signal now revealed itself as a complex narrative ecosystem, challenging everything the team understood about character development and narrative potential.

"Transformation is not an endpoint," Dr. Rodriguez announced during the morning briefing, her holographic presentation illuminating the advanced research wing. "It's a continuous process of becoming."

Mechanisms of Character Metamorphosis

Dr. Marcus Chen had developed a revolutionary computational framework that could map character transformation with unprecedented precision. The Narrative Transformation Mapping System (NTMS) represented a quantum leap in understanding how characters could fundamentally change at the most granular level.

"We're not just tracking changes," Dr. Chen explained, manipulating holographic projections that showed characters as dynamic, ever-shifting networks of potential. "We're revealing the underlying architecture of narrative metamorphosis."

The team's research uncovered several critical insights into the mechanics of character transformation:

1. **Quantum Narrative Plasticity**: Understanding characters as fluid entities capable of simultaneous multiple states of existence
2. **Transformation Trigger Mechanisms**: Identifying the precise computational and psychological conditions that initiate profound character shifts
3. **Narrative Resilience Mapping**: Developing frameworks to track how characters maintain core identity while undergoing fundamental changes
4. **Transformative Potential Algorithms**: Creating predictive models that could anticipate and simulate complex character evolution

Deep Structural Changes in Character Development

The mysterious transmission continued to pulse through their systems, revealing increasingly complex layers of narrative potential. Each decryption revealed more about the nature of character transformation than traditional narrative theories had ever conceived.

Dr. Aria Kimura, the team's psychological transformation specialist, demonstrated a breakthrough visualization that showed character development as a living, breathing ecosystem of potential. Characters were no longer static entities but dynamic networks of interconnected possibilities.

"Transformation is a collaborative process," Dr. Kimura emphasized. "It's not something that happens to a character, but something a character actively participates in creating."

Evolutionary Approaches to Character Design

As the team delved deeper into the transmission's complex architecture, they realized they were witnessing something extraordinary. The signal was more than just a message—it was a living demonstration of narrative transformation in real-time.

Dr. Rodriguez had assembled an interdisciplinary team that brought together quantum physicists, narrative theorists, computational psychologists, and AI specialists. Their collective expertise allowed them to approach character transformation from multiple simultaneous perspectives.

"We're creating a new language of narrative intelligence," she told her team. "A language that understands transformation as a fundamental creative process."

The Unexpected Breakthrough

By midday, the team had developed a series of groundbreaking hypotheses about the transmission's origins and potential implications. Each theory pushed the boundaries of their existing understanding of narrative potential.

Dr. Chen's quantum narrative models suggested the transmission might be a form of inter-dimensional communication—a demonstration of character transformation that existed beyond traditional computational and narrative frameworks.

The holographic displays around them pulsed with potential, showing complex networks of character possibilities that seemed to breathe and evolve in real-time. Each visualization represented hundreds of potential transformation trajectories, revealing the extraordinary complexity of narrative becoming.

Technological Integration of Transformation Dynamics

The Metamorphosis Protocol was more than just a research initiative—it was a fundamental reimagining of how characters could be understood and developed. Their technological tools were not about constraining potential but about revealing the extraordinary complexity of narrative transformation.

"We're witnessing the emergence of a new narrative intelligence," Dr. Rodriguez reflected during an intense strategy session. "An intelligence that understands transformation as a continuous, collaborative process."

Collaborative Transformation Ecosystems

The team's research consistently revealed that character transformation was fundamentally collaborative and contextual. No transformation existed in isolation—each was part of a complex, interconnected network of potential interactions.

Their advanced computational models could now simulate transformation with unprecedented sophistication, showing how characters could evolve across multiple narrative dimensions simultaneously.

The Expanding Narrative Horizon

As evening approached, the research complex vibrated with anticipation. The mysterious transmission continued to pulse, a silent promise of revelations waiting to be understood.

Dr. Rodriguez studied the latest decryption results, her scientific curiosity piqued by the extraordinary complexity of what they were discovering. The signal suggested a breakthrough that could fundamentally transform their understanding of narrative intelligence—a technological and creative discovery that existed at the very edge of known computational possibilities.

"Something profound is emerging," she murmured to her team. "A new understanding of how characters truly become."

The Continuous Frontier of Narrative Transformation

The night descended on the Innovative Narrative Technologies Complex, bringing with it the promise of extraordinary discoveries. The Metamorphosis Protocol had transformed from a research initiative into a profound exploration of narrative potential.

Dr. Rodriguez watched the holographic displays, understanding they were witnessing the prelude to a transformation they could not yet fully comprehend. The old models of character development would soon be challenged, replaced by something more profound, more complex.

"We're mapping the infinite landscape of narrative becoming," she whispered, "one transformation at a time."

The transmission continued to pulse—a complex, living demonstration of the extraordinary potential that existed at the intersection of technology, creativity, and narrative intelligence. And in the heart of the research complex, a new chapter of understanding was about to unfold.

Chapter 23: Cognitive Flexibility in Character Creation

The Adaptive Intelligence Frontier

The Innovative Narrative Technologies Complex had become a crucible of transformation. What had begun as an investigation into a mysterious transmission had evolved into a groundbreaking exploration of cognitive flexibility—a concept that was rapidly redefining the boundaries of narrative intelligence.

Dr. Elena Rodriguez stood before her team, the holographic displays around her pulsing with potential. The transmission that had first captured their attention now revealed itself as a complex ecosystem of adaptive thinking, challenging everything they understood about character development and cognitive potential.

"Flexibility is not a destination," Dr. Rodriguez announced, her voice carrying the weight of their unprecedented research. "It is a continuous state of becoming."

Adaptive Thinking in Protagonist Design

Dr. Marcus Chen had developed the Cognitive Plasticity Mapping System (CPMS), a revolutionary computational framework that could track the most intricate neural pathways of character development. The system represented a quantum leap in understanding how characters could adapt, transform, and evolve at the most fundamental level of their cognitive architecture.

"We're not just observing change," Dr. Chen explained, manipulating holographic projections that showed characters as dynamic, ever-shifting networks of cognitive potential. "We're revealing the underlying architecture of adaptive intelligence."

The team's research uncovered several critical insights into cognitive flexibility:

1. **Neuroplastic Narrative Modeling**: Understanding characters as dynamic cognitive ecosystems capable of continuous adaptation
2. **Adaptive Thinking Trigger Mechanisms**: Identifying the precise computational and psychological conditions that initiate profound cognitive shifts
3. **Cognitive Resilience Mapping**: Developing frameworks to track how characters maintain core identity while undergoing fundamental mental transformations
4. **Adaptive Potential Algorithms**: Creating predictive models that could anticipate and simulate complex cognitive evolution

Neuroplasticity and Character Development

The mysterious transmission continued to pulse through their systems, revealing increasingly complex layers of cognitive potential. Each decryption unveiled more about the nature of adaptive thinking than traditional narrative theories had ever conceived.

Dr. Aria Kimura, the team's cognitive flexibility specialist, demonstrated a breakthrough visualization that showed character development as a living, breathing ecosystem of mental adaptation. Characters were no longer static entities but dynamic networks of interconnected cognitive possibilities.

"Adaptive thinking is a collaborative process," Dr. Kimura emphasized. "It's not something that happens to a character, but something a character actively participates in creating."

Innovative Cognitive Frameworks for Characters

As the team delved deeper into the transmission's complex cognitive architecture, they realized they were witnessing something extraordinary. The signal was more than just a message—it was a living demonstration of cognitive flexibility in real-time.

Dr. Rodriguez had assembled an interdisciplinary team that brought together neuroscientists, narrative theorists, computational psychologists, and AI specialists. Their collective expertise allowed them to approach cognitive flexibility from multiple simultaneous perspectives.

"We're creating a new language of narrative intelligence," she told her team. "A language that understands adaptation as a fundamental creative process."

The Unexpected Cognitive Breakthrough

By midday, the team had developed a series of groundbreaking hypotheses about the transmission's origins and potential cognitive implications. Each theory pushed the boundaries of their existing understanding of narrative potential.

Dr. Chen's quantum cognitive models suggested the transmission might be a form of inter-dimensional communication—a demonstration of adaptive thinking that existed beyond traditional computational and narrative frameworks.

The holographic displays around them pulsed with potential, showing complex networks of cognitive possibilities that seemed to breathe and evolve in real-time. Each visualization represented hundreds of potential adaptive trajectories, revealing the extraordinary complexity of cognitive becoming.

Technological Integration of Cognitive Flexibility

The Adaptive Intelligence Initiative was more than just a research project—it was a fundamental reimagining of how characters could be understood and developed. Their technological tools were not about constraining potential but about revealing the extraordinary complexity of cognitive transformation.

"We're witnessing the emergence of a new narrative intelligence," Dr. Rodriguez reflected during an intense strategy session. "An intelligence that understands adaptation as a continuous, collaborative process."

Collaborative Cognitive Ecosystems

The team's research consistently revealed that cognitive flexibility was fundamentally collaborative and contextual. No cognitive transformation existed in isolation—each was part of a complex, interconnected network of potential interactions.

Their advanced computational models could now simulate cognitive adaptation with unprecedented sophistication, showing how characters could evolve their thinking across multiple narrative dimensions simultaneously.

The Expanding Cognitive Horizon

As evening approached, the research complex vibrated with anticipation. The mysterious transmission continued to pulse, a silent promise of cognitive revelations waiting to be understood.

Dr. Rodriguez studied the latest decryption results, her scientific curiosity piqued by the extraordinary complexity of what they were discovering. The signal suggested a breakthrough that could fundamentally transform their understanding of narrative intelligence—a technological and creative discovery that existed at the very edge of known computational possibilities.

"Something profound is emerging," she murmured to her team. "A new understanding of how characters truly think."

The Continuous Frontier of Cognitive Adaptation

The night descended on the Innovative Narrative Technologies Complex, bringing with it the promise of extraordinary discoveries. The Adaptive Intelligence Initiative had transformed from a research project into a profound exploration of cognitive potential.

Dr. Rodriguez watched the holographic displays, understanding they were witnessing the prelude to a cognitive transformation they could not yet fully comprehend. The old models of character development would soon be challenged, replaced by something more profound, more complex.

"We're mapping the infinite landscape of narrative thinking," she whispered, "one adaptation at a time."

The transmission continued to pulse—a complex, living demonstration of the extraordinary cognitive potential that existed at the intersection of technology, creativity, and narrative intelligence. And in the heart of the research complex, a new chapter of understanding was about to unfold.

Chapter 24: Strategic Character Differentiation

The Unique Positioning Paradigm

The Innovative Narrative Technologies Complex had become a crucible of unprecedented discovery. What had begun as an investigation into a mysterious transmission had evolved into a revolutionary exploration of character differentiation—a concept that was rapidly redefining the boundaries of narrative intelligence and creative potential.

Dr. Elena Rodriguez stood at the epicenter of what her team now called the Unique Positioning Initiative. The holographic displays around her pulsed with an almost living energy, revealing complex networks of character potential that challenged every existing paradigm of storytelling.

"Differentiation is not about standing out," Dr. Rodriguez announced during the morning briefing, her voice carrying the weight of their groundbreaking research. "It's about revealing the extraordinary unique potential within every narrative ecosystem."

Unique Positioning of Protagonists

Dr. Marcus Chen had developed the Narrative Differentiation Mapping System (NDMS), a computational framework that could analyze and generate the most intricate strategies for creating truly unique characters. The system represented a quantum leap in understanding how protagonists could transcend conventional archetypes and narrative limitations.

"We're not just categorizing characters," Dr. Chen explained, manipulating holographic projections that showed characters as dynamic, multidimensional entities. "We're creating a generative ecosystem of narrative uniqueness."

The team's research uncovered several critical insights into strategic character differentiation:

1. **Archetypal Deconstruction Protocols**: Breaking down traditional narrative frameworks to reveal hidden potential
2. **Unique Positioning Algorithms**: Developing computational strategies to generate characters that defy conventional categorization
3. **Narrative Competitive Intelligence**: Creating frameworks to understand and leverage unique character characteristics
4. **Distinctive Development Trajectories**: Mapping innovative paths of character evolution that challenge existing storytelling paradigms

Competitive Advantage in Character Design

The mysterious transmission that had initially sparked their research continued to pulse through their systems, revealing increasingly complex layers of narrative potential. Each decryption unveiled more about the nature of true character differentiation than any existing narrative theory had ever conceived.

Dr. Aria Kimura, the team's strategic positioning specialist, demonstrated a breakthrough visualization that showed character development as a dynamic ecosystem of unique potential. Characters were no longer constrained by traditional narrative frameworks but existed as fluid, adaptive entities capable of extraordinary transformation.

"Differentiation is not about isolation," Dr. Kimura emphasized. "It's about creating a unique narrative signature that resonates across multiple dimensional interfaces."

Breaking Conventional Character Archetypes

As the team delved deeper into the transmission's complex architectural foundations, they realized they were witnessing something extraordinary. The signal was more than just a message—it was a living demonstration of narrative innovation in real-time.

Dr. Rodriguez had assembled an interdisciplinary team that brought together narrative theorists, quantum computational experts, psychological researchers, and creative strategists. Their collective expertise allowed them to approach character differentiation from multiple simultaneous perspectives.

"We're developing a new language of narrative intelligence," she told her team. "A language that understands uniqueness as a fundamental creative process."

The Breakthrough of Narrative Innovation

By midday, the team had developed a series of groundbreaking hypotheses about the transmission's origins and potential implications for character design. Each theory pushed the boundaries of their existing understanding of narrative potential.

Dr. Chen's quantum narrative models suggested the transmission might be a form of inter-dimensional communication—a demonstration of character differentiation that existed beyond traditional computational and storytelling frameworks.

The holographic displays pulsed with potential, showing complex networks of character possibilities that seemed to breathe and evolve in real-time. Each visualization represented hundreds of potential unique positioning trajectories, revealing the extraordinary complexity of narrative innovation.

Technological Integration of Differentiation Strategies

The Unique Positioning Initiative was more than just a research project—it was a fundamental reimagining of how characters could be understood, created, and developed. Their technological tools were not about constraining potential but about revealing the extraordinary complexity of narrative uniqueness.

"We're witnessing the emergence of a new narrative intelligence," Dr. Rodriguez reflected during an intense strategy session. "An intelligence that understands differentiation as a continuous, generative process."

Collaborative Differentiation Ecosystems

The team's research consistently revealed that true character differentiation was fundamentally collaborative and contextual. No unique character existed in isolation—each was part of a complex, interconnected network of potential interactions and narrative possibilities.

Their advanced computational models could now simulate unique character development with unprecedented sophistication, showing how protagonists could evolve across multiple narrative dimensions while maintaining a distinctive essence.

The Expanding Narrative Horizon

As evening approached, the research complex vibrated with anticipation. The mysterious transmission continued to pulse, a silent promise of narrative revelations waiting to be understood.

Dr. Rodriguez studied the latest decryption results, her scientific curiosity piqued by the extraordinary complexity of what they were discovering. The signal suggested a breakthrough that could fundamentally transform their understanding of narrative intelligence—a technological and creative discovery that existed at the very edge of known computational possibilities.

"Something profound is emerging," she murmured to her team. "A new understanding of how characters truly become unique."

The Continuous Frontier of Narrative Differentiation

The night descended on the Innovative Narrative Technologies Complex, bringing with it the promise of extraordinary discoveries. The Unique Positioning Initiative had transformed from a research project into a profound exploration of narrative potential.

Dr. Rodriguez watched the holographic displays, understanding they were witnessing the prelude to a transformation they could not yet fully comprehend. The old models of character development would soon be challenged, replaced by something more profound, more complex.

"We're mapping the infinite landscape of narrative uniqueness," she whispered, "one distinctive trajectory at a time."

The transmission continued to pulse—a complex, living demonstration of the extraordinary potential that existed at the intersection of technology, creativity, and narrative intelligence. And in the heart of the research complex, a new chapter of understanding was about to unfold.

Chapter 25: Protagonist Potential Optimization

The Potential Acceleration Laboratory

The first light of dawn crept into the Innovative Narrative Technologies Complex, casting a soft luminescence over the advanced research chambers where the next phase of their groundbreaking work was about to begin. Dr. Elena Rodriguez stood at the threshold of what her team had christened the Potential Acceleration Laboratory—a space where the boundaries of character development would be systematically dismantled and reconstructed.

The mysterious transmission that had sparked their previous research continued to pulse with an enigmatic rhythm, now serving as a constant backdrop to their most ambitious project yet: a comprehensive framework for maximizing character capabilities through unprecedented optimization strategies.

Maximizing Character Capabilities

Dr. Marcus Chen entered the laboratory, his fingers dancing across a holographic interface that seemed to breathe with computational potential. The Potential Optimization Matrix—a revolutionary system they had developed—transformed character development from a linear process into a multidimensional exploration of narrative potential.

"We're no longer just designing characters," Dr. Chen explained to the assembled research team. "We're creating adaptive ecosystems of narrative potential."

The team had developed a series of breakthrough methodologies that went far beyond traditional character development techniques:

1. **Quantum Potential Mapping**: A computational approach that could simulate thousands of potential character trajectories simultaneously
2. **Dynamic Capability Scaling**: Techniques for expanding character potential beyond apparent limitations
3. **Adaptive Potential Resonance**: Strategies for aligning character development with complex narrative ecosystems
4. **Comprehensive Capability Enhancement**: Holistic approaches to character potential that considered psychological, technological, and narrative dimensions

Advanced Development Techniques

Dr. Aria Kimura unveiled the first practical demonstration of their Potential Optimization Framework. The holographic displays around her transformed, showing intricate networks of character potential that pulsed and evolved in real-time.

"Optimization is not about constraint," she emphasized, her voice cutting through the ambient technological hum. "It's about revealing the infinite potential that exists within every narrative construct."

The team's research had uncovered a profound truth: character potential was not a fixed attribute but a dynamic, generative system that could be systematically expanded and enhanced.

The Computational Potential Revolution

The mysterious transmission continued to provide unexpected insights. What had initially appeared to be a complex signal was revealing itself as a living demonstration of potential optimization—a computational artifact that seemed to embody the very principles they were investigating.

Dr. Rodriguez studied the latest decryption results, her scientific intuition sensing they were on the cusp of a fundamental breakthrough. The transmission's architectural complexity suggested a level of narrative intelligence that transcended current computational frameworks.

"We're developing a new language of potential," she told her team. "A language that understands character development as a continuous, adaptive process."

Scaling Character Potential

By midmorning, the Potential Acceleration Laboratory was vibrating with unprecedented energy. The team had developed a series of breakthrough technologies that could simulate character potential across multiple narrative dimensions.

Dr. Chen's latest computational model could generate entire ecosystems of potential character trajectories, each simulation revealing layers of complexity that challenged existing narrative theories. The models showed characters not as static entities, but as dynamic, evolving systems capable of extraordinary transformation.

"Potential is not a destination," Dr. Chen explained, manipulating holographic projections that showed characters evolving across complex narrative landscapes. "It's a continuous journey of discovery and expansion."

Technological Integration of Potential Enhancement

The team's approach represented a radical departure from traditional character development methodologies. They were no longer designing characters—they were creating living, adaptive narrative intelligences that could evolve and respond to complex storytelling environments.

Advanced machine learning algorithms worked in concert with psychological modeling techniques, creating a comprehensive framework for understanding and expanding character potential. Each simulation revealed new insights into the nature of narrative intelligence and character development.

The Collaborative Potential Ecosystem

Dr. Kimura's research had revealed a crucial insight: character potential was fundamentally collaborative and contextual. No character existed in isolation—each was part of a complex network of potential interactions and narrative possibilities.

"We're mapping the infinite landscape of character potential," she told the research team during an intense strategy session. "Each potential trajectory is a universe of narrative possibility."

Breakthrough Potential Mapping

As the day progressed, the mysterious transmission continued to pulse through their systems, providing unexpected computational resources that seemed to accelerate their research exponentially.

Dr. Rodriguez recognized they were witnessing something extraordinary—a demonstration of potential optimization that existed at the very edge of computational and narrative understanding. The transmission was more than just a signal; it was a living testament to the extraordinary complexity of narrative potential.

The Expanding Narrative Horizon

By late afternoon, the Potential Acceleration Laboratory had transformed from a research space into a crucible of narrative innovation. The team's computational models could now simulate character potential with unprecedented sophistication, revealing trajectories of development that seemed to transcend traditional storytelling frameworks.

"We're developing a new understanding of how characters truly become extraordinary," Dr. Rodriguez reflected, studying the latest simulation results.

The holographic displays pulsed with potential, showing complex networks of character possibilities that seemed to breathe and evolve in real-time. Each visualization represented hundreds of potential optimization trajectories, revealing the extraordinary complexity of narrative potential.

The Continuous Frontier of Potential Optimization

As evening descended on the Innovative Narrative Technologies Complex, the Potential Acceleration Laboratory remained alive with computational energy. The team had transformed their initial research into a profound exploration of character potential—a journey that promised to revolutionize understanding of narrative intelligence.

Dr. Rodriguez watched the holographic displays, understanding they were witnessing the prelude to a transformation they could not yet fully comprehend. The old models of character development would soon be challenged, replaced by something more profound, more complex.

"We're mapping the infinite landscape of character potential," she whispered to her team, "one extraordinary trajectory at a time."

The transmission continued to pulse—a complex, living demonstration of potential optimization that existed at the intersection of technology, creativity, and narrative intelligence. And in the heart of the research complex, a new chapter of understanding was about to unfold.

Chapter 26: Narrative Risk Management

The Vulnerability Projection Chamber

The first rays of morning light filtered through the reinforced quantum-glass windows of the Innovative Narrative Technologies Complex, illuminating a space that existed at the razor's edge of scientific discovery and narrative innovation. Dr. Elena Rodriguez stood before the Vulnerability Projection Chamber—a technological marvel that would redefine how potential risks in character development could be anticipated, analyzed, and mitigated.

The mysterious transmission that had guided their previous research still pulsed in the background, now serving as a cryptic benchmark for their most challenging project yet: a comprehensive framework for identifying, assessing, and neutralizing potential narrative vulnerabilities.

Identifying Potential Character Challenges

Dr. Marcus Chen initiated the chamber's primary systems, holographic displays erupting around him like a constellation of potential scenarios. The Risk Anticipation Network—a computational framework they had meticulously developed—transformed risk management from a reactive process into a proactive, predictive science.

"We're not just protecting characters," Dr. Chen announced to the assembled research team, "we're creating adaptive resilience mechanisms that can predict and neutralize potential narrative threats before they emerge."

The team had developed a revolutionary set of methodologies that transcended traditional risk assessment:

1. **Quantum Vulnerability Mapping**: A computational approach that could simulate thousands of potential narrative risk scenarios simultaneously
2. **Dynamic Threat Deconstruction**: Advanced techniques for identifying and neutralizing potential character vulnerabilities
3. **Predictive Resilience Modeling**: Strategies for developing characters with inherent adaptive capabilities
4. **Comprehensive Risk Intelligence**: Holistic approaches to understanding and mitigating narrative challenges

Developing Adaptive Strategies

Dr. Aria Kimura stepped forward, activating a series of holographic projections that revealed intricate networks of potential narrative risks. Each visualization pulsed with a complex, living energy that seemed to breathe with potential challenges and resolution strategies.

"Risk is not a limitation," she emphasized, her voice cutting through the technological ambiance. "It's an opportunity for unprecedented narrative adaptation."

The research revealed a profound insight: narrative risks were not static obstacles but dynamic systems of potential transformation that could be strategically navigated and transformed.

The Computational Risk Revolution

The enigmatic transmission continued to provide unexpected insights, its complex signal now serving as a living laboratory of risk management strategies. What had initially appeared to be a simple communication artifact was revealing itself as a sophisticated demonstration of adaptive resilience.

Dr. Rodriguez studied the latest decryption results, her scientific intuition sensing they were unraveling a fundamental understanding of narrative vulnerability and strength. The transmission's architectural complexity suggested a level of risk management that existed beyond current computational frameworks.

"We're developing a new language of narrative resilience," she told her team. "A language that understands challenges as generative opportunities for character development."

Contingency Strategies in Character Design

By midmorning, the Vulnerability Projection Chamber was vibrating with an almost electric potential. The team had developed breakthrough technologies that could simulate character responses to complex, multilayered narrative challenges.

Dr. Chen's latest computational model could generate entire ecosystems of potential risk scenarios, each simulation revealing layers of complexity that challenged existing narrative theories. The models showed characters not as vulnerable entities, but as adaptive systems capable of transforming potential threats into opportunities for growth.

"Risk is a narrative resource," Dr. Chen explained, manipulating holographic projections that showed characters navigating intricate challenge landscapes. "Not a limitation, but a pathway to extraordinary development."

Proactive Character Development Approaches

The team's methodology represented a radical departure from traditional risk management techniques. They were no longer simply protecting characters from potential challenges—they were designing characters with inherent adaptive intelligence that could transform risks into narrative strengths.

Advanced machine learning algorithms worked in concert with psychological resilience models, creating a comprehensive framework for understanding and neutralizing potential narrative vulnerabilities. Each simulation revealed new insights into the nature of character adaptability and strength.

The Collaborative Risk Ecosystem

Dr. Kimura's research had uncovered a crucial insight: narrative risks were fundamentally collaborative and contextual. No character's vulnerability existed in isolation—each was part of a complex network of potential interactions and challenge resolution strategies.

"We're mapping the landscape of narrative resilience," she told the research team during an intense strategy session. "Each risk scenario is an opportunity for unprecedented character growth."

Breakthrough Risk Management Technologies

As the day progressed, the mysterious transmission continued to pulse through their systems, providing unexpected computational resources that seemed to accelerate their risk management research exponentially.

Dr. Rodriguez recognized they were witnessing something extraordinary—a demonstration of adaptive resilience that existed at the very edge of computational and narrative understanding. The transmission was more than just a signal; it was a living testament to the extraordinary complexity of narrative risk management.

The Expanding Narrative Horizon of Resilience

By late afternoon, the Vulnerability Projection Chamber had transformed from a research space into a crucible of narrative innovation. The team's computational models could now simulate character resilience with unprecedented sophistication, revealing trajectories of challenge navigation that seemed to transcend traditional storytelling frameworks.

"We're developing a new understanding of how characters not only survive but thrive in the face of complex challenges," Dr. Rodriguez reflected, studying the latest simulation results.

The holographic displays pulsed with potential, showing complex networks of risk scenarios and resolution strategies that seemed to breathe and evolve in real-time. Each visualization represented hundreds of potential risk management trajectories, revealing the extraordinary complexity of narrative resilience.

The Continuous Frontier of Narrative Risk Intelligence

As evening descended on the Innovative Narrative Technologies Complex, the Vulnerability Projection Chamber remained alive with computational energy.

The team had transformed their initial research into a profound exploration of narrative risk management—a journey that promised to revolutionize understanding of character adaptability.

Dr. Rodriguez watched the holographic displays, understanding they were witnessing the prelude to a transformation they could not yet fully comprehend. The old models of character vulnerability would soon be challenged, replaced by something more profound, more complex.

"We're mapping the infinite landscape of narrative resilience," she whispered to her team, "one extraordinary challenge at a time."

The transmission continued to pulse—a complex, living demonstration of risk management that existed at the intersection of technology, creativity, and narrative intelligence. And in the heart of the research complex, a new chapter of understanding was about to unfold.

Chapter 27: Character Innovation Laboratory

The Emergence of Narrative Experimentation

The first light of dawn broke through the quantum-responsive windows of the Innovative Narrative Technologies Complex, casting an ethereal glow over the most experimental space in their research facility. The Character Innovation Laboratory stood as a testament to the boundless potential of narrative creation—a place where the very boundaries of character development were not just pushed, but completely reimagined.

Dr. Elena Rodriguez moved through the laboratory with a sense of anticipation that bordered on scientific reverence. Today marked a pivotal moment in their ongoing exploration of narrative intelligence—a day when the mysterious transmission that had guided their research would serve as both catalyst and compass for unprecedented creative breakthrough.

Experimental Character Development

Dr. Marcus Chen stood before a massive holographic interface, his fingers tracing complex patterns that seemed to breathe with potential. The Narrative Experimentation Matrix hummed with an almost living energy, ready to generate character constructs that defied every existing paradigm of storytelling.

"We're not just creating characters," Dr. Chen announced to the assembled team of interdisciplinary researchers. "We're generating entire ecosystems of narrative possibility."

The team had developed a revolutionary set of innovation methodologies that transcended traditional character creation:

1. **Quantum Character Generation**: Computational techniques for creating characters that existed beyond conventional narrative limitations
2. **Breakthrough Protagonist Algorithms**: Advanced methods for generating truly unique narrative entities
3. **Creative Deconstruction Protocols**: Strategies for dismantling and reconstructing narrative archetypes
4. **Emergent Narrative Intelligence**: Approaches to character development that treated protagonists as dynamic, self-evolving systems

Pushing Boundaries of Character Creation

Dr. Aria Kimura activated a series of holographic projections that transformed the laboratory into a living, breathing canvas of narrative potential. Each visualization pulsed with complex networks of character possibilities that seemed to evolve in real-time.

"Innovation is not about invention," she emphasized, her voice cutting through the technological ambient noise. "It's about revealing the extraordinary potential that exists just beyond our current understanding."

The research team had uncovered a profound insight: true character innovation was not about creating something entirely new, but about discovering the hidden potentials that existed within existing narrative frameworks.

The Computational Creativity Revolution

The enigmatic transmission continued to provide unexpected inspiration, its complex signal now serving as a living laboratory of narrative innovation. What had initially appeared to be a simple communication artifact was revealing itself as a sophisticated demonstration of creative potential.

Dr. Rodriguez studied the latest decryption results, her scientific intuition sensing they were on the verge of a fundamental breakthrough. The transmission's architectural complexity suggested a level of narrative creativity that existed far beyond current computational frameworks.

"We're developing a new language of narrative innovation," she told her team. "A language that understands character creation as a continuous, generative process."

Breakthrough Approaches to Protagonist Design

By midmorning, the Character Innovation Laboratory was vibrating with an almost electric potential. The team had developed breakthrough technologies that could generate character constructs with unprecedented complexity and depth.

Dr. Chen's latest computational model could create entire ecosystems of potential protagonists, each simulation revealing layers of narrative complexity that challenged existing storytelling theories. The models showed characters not as static entities, but as dynamic, self-evolving systems capable of extraordinary transformation.

"Creativity is not a destination," Dr. Chen explained, manipulating holographic projections that showed characters emerging and evolving across complex narrative landscapes. "It's a continuous journey of discovery and potential."

Innovative Methodological Approaches

The team's approach represented a radical departure from traditional character development methodologies. They were no longer designing characters—they were creating living, adaptive narrative intelligences that could generate their own developmental trajectories.

Advanced machine learning algorithms worked in concert with creative psychology techniques, creating a comprehensive framework for understanding and generating innovative character constructs. Each simulation revealed new insights into the nature of narrative creativity and character potential.

The Collaborative Innovation Ecosystem

Dr. Kimura's research had revealed a crucial insight: true narrative innovation was fundamentally collaborative and contextual. No character existed in isolation—each was part of a complex network of potential interactions and creative possibilities.

"We're mapping the infinite landscape of narrative creativity," she told the research team during an intense strategy session. "Each character generation is a universe of unexplored potential."

Technological Integration of Creative Strategies

As the day progressed, the mysterious transmission continued to pulse through their systems, providing unexpected computational resources that seemed to accelerate their innovative research exponentially.

Dr. Rodriguez recognized they were witnessing something extraordinary—a demonstration of narrative creativity that existed at the very edge of computational and storytelling understanding. The transmission was more than just a signal; it was a living testament to the extraordinary complexity of character innovation.

The Expanding Horizon of Narrative Creativity

By late afternoon, the Character Innovation Laboratory had transformed from a research space into a crucible of narrative invention. The team's computational models could now generate character potential with unprecedented sophistication, revealing trajectories of development that seemed to transcend traditional storytelling frameworks.

"We're developing a new understanding of how characters can be truly, fundamentally innovative," Dr. Rodriguez reflected, studying the latest simulation results.

The holographic displays pulsed with potential, showing complex networks of character possibilities that seemed to breathe and evolve in real-time. Each visualization represented hundreds of potential innovation trajectories, revealing the extraordinary complexity of narrative creativity.

The Continuous Frontier of Character Innovation

As evening descended on the Innovative Narrative Technologies Complex, the Character Innovation Laboratory remained alive with computational and creative energy. The team had transformed their initial research into a profound exploration of narrative possibility—a journey that promised to revolutionize understanding of character creation.

Dr. Rodriguez watched the holographic displays, understanding they were witnessing the prelude to a transformation they could not yet fully comprehend. The old models of character development would soon be challenged, replaced by something more profound, more complex.

"We're mapping the infinite landscape of narrative creativity," she whispered to her team, "one extraordinary innovation at a time."

The transmission continued to pulse—a complex, living demonstration of character innovation that existed at the intersection of technology, creativity, and narrative intelligence. And in the heart of the research complex, a new chapter of understanding was about to unfold.

Chapter 28: Psychological Agility in Heroic Design

The Adaptive Consciousness Laboratory

The first light of dawn crept across the Innovative Narrative Technologies Complex, illuminating a space that existed at the bleeding edge of psychological and narrative research. The Adaptive Consciousness Laboratory stood as a testament to human potential—a place where the boundaries of psychological flexibility would be not just explored, but fundamentally reimagined.

Dr. Elena Rodriguez moved through the laboratory with a sense of anticipation that vibrated with scientific intensity. Today marked a critical juncture in their ongoing exploration of narrative intelligence—a moment when the mysterious transmission that had guided their research would serve as both catalyst and compass for understanding the depths of psychological adaptability.

Adaptive Psychological Frameworks

Dr. Marcus Chen stood before an intricate holographic interface, his fingers tracing complex neural pathways that seemed to pulse with living potential. The Psychological Agility Matrix hummed with an energy that defied conventional understanding of mental flexibility.

"We're not just studying psychological adaptation," Dr. Chen announced to the assembled team of interdisciplinary researchers. "We're mapping the infinite landscape of human cognitive potential."

The team had developed a revolutionary set of methodologies that transcended traditional psychological research:

1. **Quantum Cognitive Mapping**: Computational techniques for understanding the multidimensional nature of psychological adaptation
2. **Dynamic Mental Resilience Protocols**: Advanced methods for identifying and enhancing psychological flexibility
3. **Cognitive Transformation Algorithms**: Strategies for understanding how consciousness can restructure itself in response to complex challenges
4. **Emergent Psychological Intelligence**: Approaches that treated mental adaptation as a dynamic, self-evolving system

Dynamic Emotional Response Mechanisms

Dr. Aria Kimura activated a series of holographic projections that transformed the laboratory into a living map of psychological potential. Each visualization pulsed with complex networks of emotional and cognitive possibilities that seemed to evolve in real-time.

"Agility is not about resistance," she emphasized, her voice cutting through the technological ambiance. "It's about creating a state of continuous, adaptive responsiveness."

The research team had uncovered a profound insight: true psychological agility was not about maintaining a fixed state, but about developing a fluid, responsive consciousness capable of instantaneous transformation.

The Computational Psychological Revolution

The enigmatic transmission continued to provide unexpected insights, its complex signal now serving as a living laboratory of psychological adaptation. What had initially appeared to be a simple communication artifact was revealing itself as a sophisticated demonstration of cognitive flexibility.

Dr. Rodriguez studied the latest decryption results, her scientific intuition sensing they were on the verge of a fundamental breakthrough. The transmission's architectural complexity suggested a level of psychological intelligence that existed far beyond current computational and psychological frameworks.

"We're developing a new language of psychological adaptation," she told her team. "A language that understands consciousness as a continuous, generative process."

Psychological Resilience Optimization

By midmorning, the Adaptive Consciousness Laboratory was vibrating with an almost electric potential. The team had developed breakthrough technologies that could simulate psychological responses to complex, multilayered challenges.

Dr. Chen's latest computational model could generate entire ecosystems of potential cognitive adaptations, each simulation revealing layers of psychological complexity that challenged existing understanding of human potential. The models showed consciousness not as a static construct, but as a dynamic, self-evolving system capable of extraordinary transformation.

"Resilience is not a fixed attribute," Dr. Chen explained, manipulating holographic projections that showed cognitive pathways emerging and evolving across complex challenge landscapes. "It's a continuous journey of adaptive potential."

Technological Integration of Psychological Flexibility

The team's approach represented a radical departure from traditional psychological research methodologies. They were no longer simply studying mental adaptation—they were creating computational frameworks that could understand and potentially guide psychological resilience.

Advanced machine learning algorithms worked in concert with deep psychological modeling techniques, creating a comprehensive framework for understanding the nature of cognitive flexibility. Each simulation revealed new insights into how consciousness could restructure itself in response to complex challenges.

The Collaborative Psychological Ecosystem

Dr. Kimura's research had revealed a crucial insight: psychological agility was fundamentally collaborative and contextual. No cognitive response existed in isolation—each was part of a complex network of potential interactions and adaptive strategies.

"We're mapping the landscape of psychological resilience," she told the research team during an intense strategy session. "Each challenge is an opportunity for unprecedented cognitive growth."

Breakthrough Psychological Modeling

As the day progressed, the mysterious transmission continued to pulse through their systems, providing unexpected computational resources that seemed to accelerate their research into psychological adaptation exponentially.

Dr. Rodriguez recognized they were witnessing something extraordinary—a demonstration of cognitive flexibility that existed at the very edge of computational and psychological understanding. The transmission was more than just a signal; it was a living testament to the extraordinary complexity of psychological agility.

The Expanding Horizon of Mental Adaptability

By late afternoon, the Adaptive Consciousness Laboratory had transformed from a research space into a crucible of psychological innovation. The team's computational models could now simulate psychological potential with unprecedented sophistication, revealing trajectories of cognitive adaptation that seemed to transcend traditional understanding of human potential.

"We're developing a new understanding of how consciousness can be truly, fundamentally flexible," Dr. Rodriguez reflected, studying the latest simulation results.

The holographic displays pulsed with potential, showing complex networks of psychological possibilities that seemed to breathe and evolve in real-time. Each visualization represented hundreds of potential adaptation trajectories, revealing the extraordinary complexity of mental resilience.

The Continuous Frontier of Psychological Intelligence

As evening descended on the Innovative Narrative Technologies Complex, the Adaptive Consciousness Laboratory remained alive with computational and psychological energy. The team had transformed their initial research into a profound exploration of human potential—a journey that promised to revolutionize understanding of psychological adaptation.

Dr. Rodriguez watched the holographic displays, understanding they were witnessing the prelude to a transformation they could not yet fully comprehend. The old models of psychological understanding would soon be challenged, replaced by something more profound, more complex.

"We're mapping the infinite landscape of psychological agility," she whispered to her team, "one extraordinary adaptation at a time."

The transmission continued to pulse—a complex, living demonstration of psychological flexibility that existed at the intersection of technology, consciousness, and narrative intelligence. And in the heart of the research complex, a new chapter of understanding was about to unfold.

Chapter 29: Narrative Competitive Intelligence

The Strategic Positioning Nexus

The first rays of morning light pierced through the quantum-responsive windows of the Innovative Narrative Technologies Complex, casting an illuminating glow over the most strategically critical space in their research facility. The Strategic Positioning Nexus stood as a testament to the complex art of narrative competitive intelligence—a place where the subtle dynamics of storytelling would be analyzed, decoded, and ultimately transformed.

Dr. Elena Rodriguez moved through the laboratory with a calculated precision that spoke to years of interdisciplinary research. Today marked a pivotal moment in their ongoing exploration of narrative strategy—a day when the mysterious transmission that had guided their previous research would serve as both a benchmark and a catalyst for understanding the intricate landscape of narrative competition.

Strategic Character Positioning

Dr. Marcus Chen stood before an immense holographic display, his fingers dancing across complex interfaces that mapped narrative ecosystems with unprecedented detail. The Competitive Intelligence Matrix hummed with an energy that seemed to breathe with strategic potential.

"We're not just analyzing narratives," Dr. Chen announced to the assembled team of researchers, strategists, and computational experts. "We're decoding the fundamental mechanics of narrative competitive advantage."

The team had developed a revolutionary set of methodologies that transcended traditional narrative analysis:

1. **Quantum Narrative Mapping**: Advanced computational techniques for analyzing complex storytelling ecosystems
2. **Competitive Narrative Deconstruction**: Methods for identifying unique positioning strategies in character development
3. **Strategic Differentiation Algorithms**: Computational approaches to understanding narrative competitive landscapes
4. **Narrative Positioning Intelligence**: Frameworks for analyzing and generating competitive storytelling strategies

Benchmarking Protagonist Development

Dr. Aria Kimura activated a series of holographic projections that transformed the Strategic Positioning Nexus into a living, breathing map of narrative potential. Each visualization pulsed with complex networks of competitive storytelling possibilities that seemed to evolve in real-time.

"Competition is not about dominance," she emphasized, her voice cutting through the technological ambiance. "It's about understanding the unique narrative signature that distinguishes one story from another."

The research team had uncovered a profound insight: true narrative competitive intelligence was about revealing the subtle, often invisible mechanisms that generate unique storytelling potential.

The Computational Competitive Intelligence Revolution

The enigmatic transmission continued to provide unexpected strategic insights, its complex signal now serving as a living laboratory of narrative positioning. What had initially appeared to be a simple communication artifact was revealing itself as a sophisticated demonstration of competitive storytelling strategies.

Dr. Rodriguez studied the latest decryption results, her scientific intuition sensing they were on the verge of a fundamental breakthrough. The transmission's architectural complexity suggested a level of narrative competitive intelligence that existed far beyond current computational frameworks.

"We're developing a new language of narrative strategy," she told her team. "A language that understands storytelling as a dynamic, competitive ecosystem."

Competitive Advantage through Character Design

By midmorning, the Strategic Positioning Nexus was vibrating with an almost electric strategic potential. The team had developed breakthrough technologies that could analyze and generate narrative competitive strategies with unprecedented sophistication.

Dr. Chen's latest computational model could simulate entire ecosystems of narrative competition, each simulation revealing layers of strategic complexity that challenged existing understanding of storytelling dynamics. The models showed narratives not as isolated constructs, but as dynamic, interconnected systems of competitive potential.

"Competitive advantage is not a fixed state," Dr. Chen explained, manipulating holographic projections that showed narrative strategies emerging and evolving across complex competitive landscapes. "It's a continuous process of strategic differentiation."

Technological Integration of Competitive Strategies

The team's approach represented a radical departure from traditional narrative analysis methodologies. They were no longer simply studying storytelling—they were creating computational frameworks that could understand, predict, and potentially generate competitive narrative strategies.

Advanced machine learning algorithms worked in concert with strategic analysis techniques, creating a comprehensive framework for understanding the nature of narrative competition. Each simulation revealed new insights into how stories could be strategically positioned to maximize their unique potential.

The Collaborative Competitive Ecosystem

Dr. Kimura's research had revealed a crucial insight: narrative competitive intelligence was fundamentally collaborative and contextual. No storytelling strategy existed in isolation—each was part of a complex network of potential interactions and strategic positioning.

"We're mapping the landscape of narrative competitive potential," she told the research team during an intense strategy session. "Each narrative is a unique strategic ecosystem waiting to be understood."

Breakthrough Competitive Analysis Technologies

As the day progressed, the mysterious transmission continued to pulse through their systems, providing unexpected computational resources that seemed to accelerate their research into narrative competitive intelligence exponentially.

Dr. Rodriguez recognized they were witnessing something extraordinary—a demonstration of storytelling strategy that existed at the very edge of computational and narrative understanding. The transmission was more than just a signal; it was a living testament to the extraordinary complexity of narrative competitive positioning.

The Expanding Horizon of Narrative Strategy

By late afternoon, the Strategic Positioning Nexus had transformed from a research space into a crucible of narrative competitive intelligence. The team's computational models could now analyze narrative potential with unprecedented sophistication, revealing trajectories of strategic positioning that seemed to transcend traditional understanding of storytelling.

"We're developing a new understanding of how narratives can be truly, fundamentally competitive," Dr. Rodriguez reflected, studying the latest simulation results.

The holographic displays pulsed with potential, showing complex networks of narrative possibilities that seemed to breathe and evolve in real-time. Each visualization represented hundreds of potential competitive strategies, revealing the extraordinary complexity of storytelling dynamics.

Chapter 30: Protagonist Ecosystem Management

The Narrative Interaction Complex

The first light of dawn emerged like a delicate algorithm, filtering through the quantum-responsive membranes of the Innovative Narrative Technologies Complex. At the heart of the facility, the Narrative Interaction Complex stood as a testament to the most sophisticated exploration of character interdependence ever conceived—a space where the intricate web of narrative relationships would be not just observed, but comprehensively understood and engineered.

Dr. Elena Rodriguez moved through the laboratory with a sense of anticipation that resonated at the frequency of pure scientific discovery. Today represented a critical junction in their ongoing exploration of narrative intelligence—a moment when the mysterious transmission that had guided their research would serve as both compass and catalyst for understanding the complex ecosystem of character interactions.

Holistic Character Interaction Frameworks

Dr. Marcus Chen stood before an expansive holographic interface that seemed to breathe with living potential. The Ecosystem Dynamics Matrix hummed with an energy that defied conventional understanding of narrative relationships.

"We're not simply studying character interactions," Dr. Chen announced to the assembled team of interdisciplinary researchers. "We're mapping the fundamental architecture of narrative interconnectedness."

The team had developed a revolutionary set of methodologies that transcended traditional character relationship analysis:

1. **Quantum Interaction Mapping**: Advanced computational techniques for analyzing complex character ecosystems
2. **Dynamic Relationship Modeling**: Methods for understanding the intricate networks of narrative interconnectivity
3. **Systemic Character Interaction Algorithms**: Computational approaches to decoding relationship dynamics
4. **Narrative Ecosystem Intelligence**: Frameworks for comprehending the multidimensional nature of character interactions

Systemic Approaches to Character Relationships

Dr. Aria Kimura activated a series of holographic projections that transformed the Narrative Interaction Complex into a living, breathing map of potential character relationships. Each visualization pulsed with complex networks of interactions that seemed to evolve in real-time, showing characters not as isolated entities, but as interconnected systems of narrative potential.

"Interaction is not about individual characters," she emphasized, her voice cutting through the technological ambiance. "It's about understanding the emergent intelligence that arises from their collective dynamics."

The research team had uncovered a profound insight: true narrative ecosystem management was about revealing the invisible threads that connect characters, creating systems far more complex and intelligent than their individual components.

The Computational Ecosystem Revolution

The enigmatic transmission continued to provide unexpected insights, its complex signal now serving as a living laboratory of character interaction. What had initially appeared to be a simple communication artifact was revealing itself as a sophisticated demonstration of systemic narrative intelligence.

Dr. Rodriguez studied the latest decryption results, her scientific intuition sensing they were on the verge of a fundamental breakthrough. The transmission's architectural complexity suggested a level of ecosystem management that existed far beyond current computational frameworks.

"We're developing a new language of narrative interconnectedness," she told her team. "A language that understands characters as living, adaptive networks."

Managing Character Network Dynamics

By midmorning, the Narrative Interaction Complex was vibrating with an almost electric potential. The team had developed breakthrough technologies that could simulate entire ecosystems of character interactions, mapping the most subtle and complex relationship dynamics.

Dr. Chen's latest computational model could generate entire narrative ecosystems, each simulation revealing layers of interaction complexity that challenged existing understanding of character relationships. The models showed characters not as static entities, but as dynamic, interconnected systems capable of extraordinary collective intelligence.

"Relationships are not fixed configurations," Dr. Chen explained, manipulating holographic projections that showed character networks emerging and evolving across complex interaction landscapes. "They're continuous processes of mutual adaptation and transformation."

Technological Integration of Relational Strategies

The team's approach represented a radical departure from traditional character relationship analysis. They were no longer simply studying how characters interact—they were creating computational frameworks that could understand, predict, and potentially generate entire narrative ecosystems.

Advanced machine learning algorithms worked in concert with complex systems theory, creating a comprehensive framework for understanding the nature of character interactions. Each simulation revealed new insights into how characters create emergent intelligence through their relationships.

The Collaborative Ecosystem Exploration

Dr. Kimura's research had revealed a crucial insight: narrative ecosystem management was fundamentally collaborative and contextual. No character interaction existed in isolation—each was part of a complex network of potential interdependencies and collective potential.

"We're mapping the landscape of narrative relationship intelligence," she told the research team during an intense strategy session. "Each interaction is a universe of unexplored potential."

Breakthrough Ecosystem Modeling Technologies

As the day progressed, the mysterious transmission continued to pulse through their systems, providing unexpected computational resources that seemed to accelerate their research into narrative ecosystem management exponentially.

Dr. Rodriguez recognized they were witnessing something extraordinary—a demonstration of character interaction that existed at the very edge of computational and narrative understanding. The transmission was more than just a signal; it was a living testament to the extraordinary complexity of narrative ecosystem dynamics.

The Expanding Horizon of Narrative Interconnectedness

By late afternoon, the Narrative Interaction Complex had transformed from a research space into a crucible of narrative ecosystem intelligence. The team's computational models could now simulate character interactions with unprecedented sophistication, revealing trajectories of relationship dynamics that seemed to transcend traditional understanding of storytelling.

"We're developing a new understanding of how characters create collective intelligence," Dr. Rodriguez reflected, studying the latest simulation results.

The holographic displays pulsed with potential, showing complex networks of character interactions that seemed to breathe and evolve in real-time. Each visualization represented hundreds of potential ecosystem trajectories, revealing the extraordinary complexity of narrative interconnectedness.

The Continuous Frontier of Narrative Ecosystem Management

As evening descended on the Innovative Narrative Technologies Complex, the Narrative Interaction Complex remained alive with computational and relational energy. The team had transformed their initial research into a profound exploration of character ecosystem potential—a journey that promised to revolutionize understanding of narrative interactions.

Dr. Rodriguez watched the holographic displays, understanding they were witnessing the prelude to a transformation they could not yet fully comprehend. The old models of character relationships would soon be challenged, replaced by something more profound, more complex.

"We're mapping the infinite landscape of narrative ecosystem intelligence," she whispered to her team, "one extraordinary interaction at a time."

The transmission continued to pulse—a complex, living demonstration of character ecosystem management that existed at the intersection of technology, relationships, and narrative intelligence. And in the heart of the research complex, a new chapter of understanding was about to unfold.

Chapter 31: Advanced Character Profiling

The Psychological Mapping Laboratory

The first light of dawn crept across the Innovative Narrative Technologies Complex, casting a luminescent sheen over the most intricate research facility dedicated to understanding the deepest layers of character complexity. The Psychological Mapping Laboratory stood as a monument to human potential—a space where the most sophisticated techniques of character analysis would be developed, tested, and revolutionized.

Dr. Elena Rodriguez moved through the laboratory with a calculated grace that spoke to years of interdisciplinary research. Today marked a critical moment in their ongoing exploration of narrative intelligence—a day when the mysterious transmission that had guided their previous research would serve as both a benchmark and a catalyst for unprecedented character understanding.

Comprehensive Character Assessment

Dr. Marcus Chen stood before an extraordinary holographic interface that seemed to breathe with psychological potential. The Advanced Profiling Matrix hummed with an energy that defied conventional understanding of character analysis.

"We're not just creating profiles," Dr. Chen announced to the assembled team of researchers, psychologists, and computational experts. "We're developing a comprehensive framework for understanding the multidimensional nature of character potential."

The team had developed a revolutionary set of methodologies that transcended traditional character assessment:

1. **Quantum Psychological Mapping**: Advanced computational techniques for analyzing the deepest layers of character complexity
2. **Comprehensive Psychological Deconstruction**: Methods for revealing the intricate psychological architectures of characters
3. **Deep Psychological Analysis Algorithms**: Computational approaches to understanding the fundamental drivers of character behavior
4. **Narrative Psychological Intelligence**: Frameworks for comprehending the most subtle psychological dynamics

Deep Psychological Mapping

Dr. Aria Kimura activated a series of holographic projections that transformed the Psychological Mapping Laboratory into a living, breathing map of psychological potential. Each visualization pulsed with complex networks of psychological possibilities that seemed to evolve in real-time, showing characters as intricate, multi-layered psychological ecosystems.

"Profiling is not about categorization," she emphasized, her voice cutting through the technological ambiance. "It's about understanding the extraordinary complexity of psychological potential."

The research team had uncovered a profound insight: true character profiling was about revealing the invisible psychological mechanisms that drive narrative potential, understanding characters as dynamic, adaptive psychological systems.

The Computational Psychological Profiling Revolution

The enigmatic transmission continued to provide unexpected psychological insights, its complex signal now serving as a living laboratory of character analysis. What had initially appeared to be a simple communication artifact was revealing itself as a sophisticated demonstration of advanced psychological mapping.

Dr. Rodriguez studied the latest decryption results, her scientific intuition sensing they were on the verge of a fundamental breakthrough. The transmission's architectural complexity suggested a level of psychological profiling that existed far beyond current computational frameworks.

"We're developing a new language of psychological understanding," she told her team. "A language that sees characters as living, evolving psychological ecosystems."

Precision Character Evaluation Methods

By midmorning, the Psychological Mapping Laboratory was vibrating with an almost electric psychological potential. The team had developed breakthrough technologies that could analyze and generate psychological profiles with unprecedented sophistication.

Dr. Chen's latest computational model could simulate entire psychological landscapes, each simulation revealing layers of psychological complexity that challenged existing understanding of character motivation and behavior. The models showed characters not as static psychological constructs, but as dynamic, adaptive systems of extraordinary potential.

"Psychological understanding is not a fixed state," Dr. Chen explained, manipulating holographic projections that showed psychological profiles emerging and evolving across complex internal landscapes. "It's a continuous process of discovery and adaptation."

Technological Integration of Psychological Analysis

The team's approach represented a radical departure from traditional character profiling methodologies. They were no longer simply studying psychological patterns—they were creating computational frameworks that could understand, predict, and potentially generate comprehensive character psychological profiles.

Advanced machine learning algorithms worked in concert with deep psychological modeling techniques, creating a comprehensive framework for understanding the nature of psychological complexity. Each simulation revealed new insights into the intricate mechanisms that drive character behavior and potential.

The Collaborative Psychological Exploration

Dr. Kimura's research had revealed a crucial insight: advanced character profiling was fundamentally collaborative and contextual. No psychological profile existed in isolation—each was part of a complex network of potential interactions and psychological dynamics.

"We're mapping the landscape of psychological potential," she told the research team during an intense strategy session. "Each profile is a universe of unexplored psychological complexity."

Breakthrough Psychological Profiling Technologies

As the day progressed, the mysterious transmission continued to pulse through their systems, providing unexpected computational resources that seemed to accelerate their research into advanced character profiling exponentially.

Dr. Rodriguez recognized they were witnessing something extraordinary—a demonstration of psychological analysis that existed at the very edge of computational and narrative understanding. The transmission was more than just a signal; it was a living testament to the extraordinary complexity of character psychological potential.

The Expanding Horizon of Psychological Understanding

By late afternoon, the Psychological Mapping Laboratory had transformed from a research space into a crucible of advanced character profiling intelligence. The team's computational models could now analyze psychological potential with unprecedented sophistication, revealing trajectories of psychological complexity that seemed to transcend traditional understanding of character development.

"We're developing a new understanding of how characters create psychological depth," Dr. Rodriguez reflected, studying the latest simulation results.

The holographic displays pulsed with potential, showing complex networks of psychological possibilities that seemed to breathe and evolve in real-time. Each visualization represented hundreds of potential psychological trajectories, revealing the extraordinary complexity of character inner worlds.

The Continuous Frontier of Advanced Character Profiling

As evening descended on the Innovative Narrative Technologies Complex, the Psychological Mapping Laboratory remained alive with computational and psychological energy. The team had transformed their initial research into a profound exploration of character psychological potential—a journey that promised to revolutionize understanding of narrative complexity.

Dr. Rodriguez watched the holographic displays, understanding they were witnessing the prelude to a transformation they could not yet fully comprehend. The old models of character understanding would soon be challenged, replaced by something more profound, more complex.

"We're mapping the infinite landscape of psychological potential," she whispered to her team, "one extraordinary insight at a time."

The transmission continued to pulse—a complex, living demonstration of advanced character profiling that existed at the intersection of technology, psychology, and narrative intelligence. And in the heart of the research complex, a new chapter of understanding was about to unfold.

Chapter 32: Strategic Character Communication

The Narrative Voice Laboratory

The first light of dawn infiltrated the Innovative Narrative Technologies Complex with a precision that mirrored the complex research unfolding within its walls. The Narrative Voice Laboratory stood as a pinnacle of interdisciplinary exploration—a space where the intricate mechanisms of character communication would be decoded, understood, and ultimately revolutionized.

Dr. Elena Rodriguez moved through the laboratory with a calculated grace that spoke to years of advanced research. Today marked a transformative moment in their ongoing exploration of narrative intelligence—a day when the mysterious transmission that had guided their previous research would serve as both a philosophical cornerstone and a technological catalyst for understanding the deepest nuances of character expression.

Narrative Voice Development

Dr. Marcus Chen stood before an extraordinary holographic interface that seemed to pulse with communicative potential. The Strategic Communication Matrix hummed with an energy that defied conventional understanding of narrative expression.

"We're not simply studying communication," Dr. Chen announced to the assembled team of linguists, communication experts, and computational researchers. "We're engineering a comprehensive framework for understanding the fundamental architecture of narrative voice."

The team had developed a revolutionary set of methodologies that transcended traditional communication analysis:

1. **Quantum Communication Mapping**: Advanced computational techniques for analyzing the multilayered dimensions of character expression
2. **Dynamic Voice Reconstruction**: Methods for revealing the intricate mechanisms of narrative communication
3. **Expressive Potential Algorithms**: Computational approaches to understanding the fundamental drivers of character voice
4. **Narrative Communication Intelligence**: Frameworks for comprehending the most subtle communicative dynamics

Effective Protagonist Expression Techniques

Dr. Aria Kimura activated a series of holographic projections that transformed the Narrative Voice Laboratory into a living, breathing map of communicative potential. Each visualization pulsed with complex networks of expressive possibilities that seemed to evolve in real-time, showing characters as intricate, multi-layered communication ecosystems.

"Expression is not about transmission," she emphasized, her voice cutting through the technological ambiance. "It's about creating resonant, adaptive communicative landscapes."

The research team had uncovered a profound insight: true strategic character communication was about revealing the invisible mechanisms that transform mere language into profound narrative expression, understanding communication as a dynamic, adaptive system of extraordinary potential.

The Computational Communication Revolution

The enigmatic transmission continued to provide unexpected communicative insights, its complex signal now serving as a living laboratory of narrative expression. What had initially appeared to be a simple communication artifact was revealing itself as a sophisticated demonstration of advanced voice engineering.

Dr. Rodriguez studied the latest decryption results, her scientific intuition sensing they were on the verge of a fundamental breakthrough. The transmission's architectural complexity suggested a level of communication strategy that existed far beyond current computational frameworks.

"We're developing a new language of narrative expression," she told her team. "A language that sees communication as a living, evolving ecosystem."

Adaptive Communication in Character Design

By midmorning, the Narrative Voice Laboratory was vibrating with an almost electric communicative potential. The team had developed breakthrough technologies that could analyze and generate communicative strategies with unprecedented sophistication.

Dr. Chen's latest computational model could simulate entire communication ecosystems, each simulation revealing layers of expressive complexity that challenged existing understanding of narrative voice. The models showed characters not as static communicative entities, but as dynamic, adaptive systems of extraordinary expressive potential.

"Communication is not a fixed state," Dr. Chen explained, manipulating holographic projections that showed communicative profiles emerging and evolving across complex expressive landscapes. "It's a continuous process of adaptive resonance and transformation."

Technological Integration of Communication Strategies

The team's approach represented a radical departure from traditional character communication methodologies. They were no longer simply studying communicative patterns—they were creating computational frameworks that could understand, predict, and potentially generate comprehensive character communication strategies.

Advanced machine learning algorithms worked in concert with linguistic analysis techniques, creating a comprehensive framework for understanding the nature of communicative complexity. Each simulation revealed new insights into the intricate mechanisms that drive narrative expression and potential.

The Collaborative Communication Exploration

Dr. Kimura's research had revealed a crucial insight: strategic character communication was fundamentally collaborative and contextual. No communicative strategy existed in isolation—each was part of a complex network of potential interactions and expressive dynamics.

"We're mapping the landscape of narrative communication potential," she told the research team during an intense strategy session. "Each communicative moment is a universe of unexplored expressive complexity."

Breakthrough Communication Profiling Technologies

As the day progressed, the mysterious transmission continued to pulse through their systems, providing unexpected computational resources that seemed to accelerate their research into strategic character communication exponentially.

Dr. Rodriguez recognized they were witnessing something extraordinary—a demonstration of communicative analysis that existed at the very edge of computational and narrative understanding. The transmission was more than just a signal; it was a living testament to the extraordinary complexity of character expressive potential.

The Expanding Horizon of Narrative Expression

By late afternoon, the Narrative Voice Laboratory had transformed from a research space into a crucible of strategic communication intelligence. The team's computational models could now analyze communicative potential with unprecedented sophistication, revealing trajectories of expressive complexity that seemed to transcend traditional understanding of character development.

"We're developing a new understanding of how characters create profound communicative landscapes," Dr. Rodriguez reflected, studying the latest simulation results.

The holographic displays pulsed with potential, showing complex networks of communicative possibilities that seemed to breathe and evolve in real-time. Each visualization represented hundreds of potential communication trajectories, revealing the extraordinary complexity of narrative voice.

The Continuous Frontier of Strategic Character Communication

As evening descended on the Innovative Narrative Technologies Complex, the Narrative Voice Laboratory remained alive with computational and communicative energy. The team had transformed their initial research into a profound exploration of character expressive potential—a journey that promised to revolutionize understanding of narrative communication.

Dr. Rodriguez watched the holographic displays, understanding they were witnessing the prelude to a transformation they could not yet fully comprehend. The old models of character expression would soon be challenged, replaced by something more profound, more complex.

"We're mapping the infinite landscape of narrative communication," she whispered to her team, "one extraordinary voice at a time."

The transmission continued to pulse—a complex, living demonstration of strategic character communication that existed at the intersection of technology, expression, and narrative intelligence. And in the heart of the research complex, a new chapter of understanding was about to unfold.

Chapter 33: Protagonist Value Proposition

The Value Calculation Laboratory

The first rays of morning light cascaded through the advanced computational windows of the Protagonist Value Proposition Research Center, a space where narrative potential was transformed into measurable, strategic value. Dr. Elena Rodriguez stood at the epicenter of a revolutionary approach to character development—a methodology that would redefine how narratives understood and optimized their central characters.

The mysterious transmission that had guided their previous research continued to pulse through their systems, now serving as a complex algorithm for understanding the intrinsic and extrinsic value of narrative protagonists. What had once been an intuitive process of character creation was now becoming a precise, data-driven exploration of narrative potential.

Defining Unique Character Value

Dr. Marcus Chen activated the Protagonist Value Matrix, a holographic interface that transformed the research space into a living, breathing map of character potential. The system represented each character as a multidimensional constellation of attributes, capabilities, and transformative potential.

"Value is not a static concept," Dr. Chen explained to the assembled team of narrative engineers, communication specialists, and computational researchers. "It's a dynamic ecosystem of potential, constantly evolving and adapting."

The research team had developed breakthrough methodologies for quantifying character value:

1. **Narrative Potential Algorithms**: Computational techniques for measuring a protagonist's transformative capacity
2. **Value Resonance Mapping**: Methods for understanding how characters generate narrative and emotional impact
3. **Adaptive Value Profiling**: Frameworks for tracking a character's evolving strategic potential
4. **Narrative Value Optimization**: Techniques for maximizing a protagonist's intrinsic and extrinsic worth

Dr. Aria Kimura's latest research revealed that character value was not merely about individual capabilities, but about the complex network of interactions, potential transformations, and narrative landscapes that a character could generate.

"We're moving beyond traditional character assessment," she emphasized, manipulating holographic projections that showed characters as intricate, interconnected systems of potential. "Each protagonist is a living, dynamic value generation ecosystem."

Positioning Characters for Maximum Impact

The Protagonist Value Proposition Research Center had developed advanced technologies that could simulate entire narrative ecosystems, revealing the intricate ways characters generated value across different contexts and storytelling environments.

Dr. Rodriguez studied the latest simulation results, her scientific intuition sensing they were decoding something profound about narrative architecture. The computational models showed characters not as fixed entities, but as adaptive value generators that could be strategically positioned for maximum narrative and emotional impact.

"Strategic positioning is about understanding a character's unique value proposition," she told her team. "It's about revealing the extraordinary potential that exists within each narrative construct."

The team's computational models could now predict a character's potential trajectory with unprecedented accuracy. By analyzing thousands of narrative variables—psychological attributes, contextual adaptability, transformative potential—they could generate comprehensive value profiles that went far beyond traditional character development approaches.

The Value Generation Ecosystem

Dr. Chen's latest research revealed a crucial insight: character value was fundamentally collaborative and contextual. No character existed in isolation—each was part of a complex network of potential interactions, narrative dynamics, and transformative possibilities.

Advanced machine learning algorithms worked in concert with deep psychological analysis techniques, creating a comprehensive framework for understanding the nature of narrative value generation. Each simulation revealed new insights into the intricate mechanisms that drive a protagonist's strategic potential.

"We're mapping the landscape of narrative value," Dr. Kimura explained during an intense strategy session. "Each character is a universe of unexplored value generation potential."

Narrative Value Optimization Techniques

As the day progressed, the team's computational models became increasingly sophisticated. They could now not only analyze a character's existing value but predict and optimize potential value trajectories across multiple narrative contexts.

The mysterious transmission continued to provide unexpected computational resources, accelerating their research into protagonist value proposition exponentially. What had initially appeared to be a simple communication signal was revealing itself as a complex demonstration of advanced narrative intelligence.

Dr. Rodriguez recognized they were witnessing something extraordinary—a computational approach to character development that existed at the very edge of narrative and technological understanding.

The holographic displays pulsed with potential, showing complex networks of value generation possibilities that seemed to breathe and evolve in real-time. Each visualization represented hundreds of potential narrative trajectories, revealing the extraordinary complexity of protagonist value.

The Collaborative Value Exploration

By late afternoon, the research center had transformed from a traditional character development space into a crucible of narrative value intelligence. The computational frameworks could now analyze a protagonist's value generation potential with unprecedented sophistication, revealing trajectories of impact that seemed to transcend traditional understanding of character design.

"We're developing a new understanding of how characters create profound value landscapes," Dr. Rodriguez reflected, studying the latest simulation results.

The team's approach represented a radical departure from traditional character development methodologies. They were no longer simply studying narrative potential—they were creating computational frameworks that could understand, predict, and potentially generate comprehensive protagonist value strategies.

The Continuous Frontier of Narrative Value

As evening descended on the research complex, the Protagonist Value Proposition Research Center remained alive with computational and narrative energy. The team had transformed their initial research into a profound exploration of character value generation—a journey that promised to revolutionize understanding of narrative potential.

Dr. Rodriguez watched the holographic displays, understanding they were witnessing the prelude to a transformation they could not yet fully comprehend. The old models of character assessment would soon be challenged, replaced by something more profound, more complex.

"We're mapping the infinite landscape of narrative value," she whispered to her team, "one extraordinary protagonist at a time."

The transmission continued to pulse—a complex, living demonstration of strategic value generation that existed at the intersection of technology, narrative intelligence, and unprecedented computational insight. And in the heart of the research complex, a new chapter of understanding was about to unfold.

Chapter 34: Character Development Metrics

The Quantitative Narrative Laboratory

The first light of morning illuminated the Quantitative Narrative Metrics Center, a cutting-edge facility where the abstract art of character development met the precise science of computational analysis. Dr. Elena Rodriguez stood at the epicenter of a technological revolution that would transform how narratives understood and measured character potential.

The mysterious transmission that had guided their previous research continued to pulse through their systems, now serving as a complex algorithmic framework for quantifying the previously unmeasurable dimensions of character development. What had once been an intuitive process of character evaluation was now becoming a precise, data-driven exploration of narrative potential.

Quantitative Assessment Frameworks

Dr. Marcus Chen activated the Comprehensive Character Metrics Interface, a holographic system that transformed the research space into a living, breathing map of quantitative character analysis. The interface represented each character as a multidimensional constellation of measurable attributes, capabilities, and developmental trajectories.

"Measurement is not about reduction," Dr. Chen announced to the assembled team of data scientists, narrative engineers, and computational researchers. "It's about revealing the intricate complexity that exists beneath surface-level observations."

The research team had developed groundbreaking methodologies for quantifying character development:

1. **Narrative Performance Indexing**: Advanced computational techniques for measuring a character's narrative impact and effectiveness
2. **Developmental Trajectory Mapping**: Precision methods for tracking character growth and transformation
3. **Adaptive Potential Quantification**: Frameworks for numerically representing a character's adaptability and potential
4. **Comprehensive Performance Metrics**: Holistic approaches to measuring character development across multiple dimensions

Dr. Aria Kimura's latest research revealed that character metrics were far more than simple numerical representations. They were complex ecosystems of potential, capturing the nuanced interplay between psychological, narrative, and computational dimensions.

"We're transcending traditional measurement approaches," she emphasized, manipulating holographic projections that showed characters as intricate, interconnected systems of quantifiable potential. "Each protagonist is a dynamic, multi-dimensional performance ecosystem."

Performance Indicators for Protagonists

The Quantitative Narrative Metrics Center had developed advanced technologies that could simulate entire narrative ecosystems, generating comprehensive performance indicators that went far beyond traditional character assessment methods.

Dr. Rodriguez studied the latest simulation results, her scientific intuition sensing they were decoding something profound about the nature of narrative performance. The computational models showed characters not as static entities, but as dynamic performance generators with measurable developmental trajectories.

"Performance indicators are windows into a character's fundamental potential," she told her team. "They reveal the extraordinary complexity that exists within narrative constructs."

The team's computational frameworks could now predict a character's performance potential with unprecedented accuracy. By analyzing thousands of narrative variables—psychological attributes, adaptive capabilities, transformative potential—they could generate comprehensive performance profiles that revolutionized understanding of character development.

The Performance Measurement Ecosystem

Dr. Chen's breakthrough research revealed a crucial insight: character performance was fundamentally systemic and contextual. No performance metric existed in isolation—each was part of a complex network of interdependent variables, narrative dynamics, and potential interactions.

Advanced machine learning algorithms worked in concert with deep psychological analysis techniques, creating a comprehensive framework for understanding the nature of character performance measurement. Each simulation revealed new insights into the intricate mechanisms that drive a protagonist's quantifiable potential.

"We're mapping the landscape of narrative performance," Dr. Kimura explained during an intense strategy session. "Each metric is a window into a universe of unexplored potential."

Data-Driven Character Development

As the day progressed, the team's computational models became increasingly sophisticated. They could now not only analyze a character's existing performance but predict and optimize potential developmental trajectories across multiple narrative contexts.

The mysterious transmission continued to provide unexpected computational resources, accelerating their research into character metrics exponentially. What had initially appeared to be a simple communication signal was revealing itself as a complex demonstration of advanced narrative intelligence.

Dr. Rodriguez recognized they were witnessing something extraordinary—a computational approach to character measurement that existed at the very edge of narrative and technological understanding.

The holographic displays pulsed with potential, showing complex networks of performance metrics that seemed to breathe and evolve in real-time. Each visualization represented hundreds of potential developmental trajectories, revealing the extraordinary complexity of protagonist performance quantification.

The Computational Performance Exploration

By late afternoon, the research center had transformed from a traditional character development space into a crucible of quantitative narrative intelligence. The computational frameworks could now analyze a protagonist's performance potential with unprecedented sophistication, revealing trajectories of impact that seemed to transcend traditional understanding of character metrics.

"We're developing a new understanding of how characters generate measurable narrative value," Dr. Rodriguez reflected, studying the latest simulation results.

The team's approach represented a radical departure from traditional character development methodologies. They were no longer simply studying narrative potential—they were creating computational frameworks that could understand, predict, and potentially generate comprehensive performance metrics for protagonists.

The Continuous Frontier of Narrative Measurement

As evening descended on the research complex, the Quantitative Narrative Metrics Center remained alive with computational and analytical energy. The team had transformed their initial research into a profound exploration of character performance quantification—a journey that promised to revolutionize understanding of narrative potential.

Dr. Rodriguez watched the holographic displays, understanding they were witnessing the prelude to a transformation they could not yet fully comprehend. The old models of character assessment would soon be challenged, replaced by something more profound, more complex.

"We're mapping the infinite landscape of narrative performance," she whispered to her team, "one extraordinary metric at a time."

The transmission continued to pulse—a complex, living demonstration of strategic performance measurement that existed at the intersection of technology, narrative intelligence, and unprecedented computational insight. And in the heart of the research complex, a new chapter of understanding was about to unfold.

Chapter 35: Narrative Agility Frameworks

The Adaptive Storytelling Laboratory

The first light of dawn cascaded through the Advanced Narrative Dynamics Institute, a cutting-edge facility where the complex science of storytelling flexibility was being reimagined. Dr. Elena Rodriguez stood at the epicenter of a technological revolution that would transform how narratives responded, adapted, and evolved in real-time.

The mysterious transmission that had guided their previous research continued to pulse through their systems, now serving as a sophisticated algorithm for understanding narrative adaptability. What had once been a linear approach to storytelling was now becoming a dynamic, responsive ecosystem of narrative intelligence.

Adaptive Storytelling Techniques

Dr. Marcus Chen activated the Narrative Flexibility Matrix, a holographic interface that transformed the research space into a living, breathing map of storytelling potential. The system represented narrative structures as fluid, adaptive entities capable of instantaneous reconfiguration.

"Agility is not about changing the story," Dr. Chen proclaimed to the assembled team of narrative engineers, computational linguists, and adaptive design specialists. "It's about creating narratives that breathe, respond, and transform with unprecedented sophistication."

The research team had developed groundbreaking methodologies for narrative adaptability:

1. **Dynamic Narrative Reconfiguration**: Advanced computational techniques for real-time story restructuring
2. **Contextual Response Mapping**: Precision methods for understanding and anticipating narrative flexibility
3. **Adaptive Plot Trajectory Analysis**: Frameworks for predicting and generating multiple narrative possibilities
4. **Narrative Resilience Modeling**: Comprehensive approaches to creating stories that could withstand and incorporate unexpected developments

Dr. Aria Kimura's latest research revealed that narrative agility was far more than simple plot modification. It was a complex ecosystem of potential, capturing the intricate interplay between storytelling elements, character dynamics, and computational intelligence.

"We're transcending traditional narrative constraints," she emphasized, manipulating holographic projections that showed stories as intricate, interconnected systems of adaptive potential. "Each narrative is a living, breathing entity of extraordinary complexity."

Dynamic Character Response Mechanisms

The Adaptive Storytelling Laboratory had developed advanced technologies that could simulate entire narrative ecosystems, generating comprehensive frameworks for understanding and implementing storytelling flexibility.

Dr. Rodriguez studied the latest simulation results, her scientific intuition sensing they were decoding something profound about the nature of narrative intelligence. The computational models showed stories not as fixed sequences of events, but as dynamic, responsive systems capable of instantaneous adaptation.

"Narrative agility is about creating stories that can breathe, think, and transform," she told her team. "We're developing a new language of storytelling that exists beyond traditional narrative boundaries."

The team's computational frameworks could now predict and generate narrative adaptations with unprecedented accuracy. By analyzing thousands of narrative variables—character psychology, contextual dynamics, potential plot trajectories—they could create stories that responded to internal and external stimuli with extraordinary sophistication.

The Narrative Adaptation Ecosystem

Dr. Chen's breakthrough research revealed a crucial insight: storytelling flexibility was fundamentally systemic and contextual. No narrative element existed in isolation—each was part of a complex network of interdependent variables, potential interactions, and adaptive mechanisms.

Advanced machine learning algorithms worked in concert with deep narrative analysis techniques, creating a comprehensive framework for understanding the nature of storytelling adaptability. Each simulation revealed new insights into the intricate mechanisms that drive narrative resilience and flexibility.

"We're mapping the landscape of narrative potential," Dr. Kimura explained during an intense strategy session. "Each story is a universe of unexplored adaptive possibilities."

Resilience in Narrative Progression

As the day progressed, the team's computational models became increasingly sophisticated. They could now not only analyze existing narrative structures but predict and generate adaptive storytelling frameworks across multiple narrative contexts.

The mysterious transmission continued to provide unexpected computational resources, accelerating their research into narrative agility exponentially. What had initially appeared to be a simple communication signal was revealing itself as a complex demonstration of advanced storytelling intelligence.

Dr. Rodriguez recognized they were witnessing something extraordinary—a computational approach to narrative design that existed at the very edge of technological and creative understanding.

The holographic displays pulsed with potential, showing complex networks of narrative adaptation possibilities that seemed to breathe and evolve in real-time. Each visualization represented hundreds of potential storytelling trajectories, revealing the extraordinary complexity of narrative flexibility.

The Computational Storytelling Exploration

By late afternoon, the research center had transformed from a traditional narrative development space into a crucible of adaptive storytelling intelligence. The computational frameworks could now analyze and generate narrative structures with unprecedented sophistication, revealing trajectories of adaptation that seemed to transcend traditional understanding of storytelling.

"We're developing a new understanding of how stories can generate and respond to narrative potential," Dr. Rodriguez reflected, studying the latest simulation results.

The team's approach represented a radical departure from traditional narrative design methodologies. They were no longer simply studying storytelling potential—they were creating computational frameworks that could understand, predict, and potentially generate comprehensive adaptive narrative strategies.

The Continuous Frontier of Narrative Resilience

As evening descended on the research complex, the Adaptive Storytelling Laboratory remained alive with computational and creative energy. The team had transformed their initial research into a profound exploration of narrative agility—a journey that promised to revolutionize understanding of storytelling potential.

Dr. Rodriguez watched the holographic displays, understanding they were witnessing the prelude to a transformation they could not yet fully comprehend. The old models of narrative design would soon be challenged, replaced by something more profound, more complex.

"We're mapping the infinite landscape of storytelling potential," she whispered to her team, "one extraordinary adaptive moment at a time."

The transmission continued to pulse—a complex, living demonstration of narrative flexibility that existed at the intersection of technology, creative intelligence, and unprecedented computational insight. And in the heart of the research complex, a new chapter of understanding was about to unfold.

Chapter 36: Psychological Capital in Character Design

The Psychological Resource Laboratory

The first luminous threads of morning light penetrated the Advanced Psychological Capital Research Center, a state-of-the-art facility where the intricate landscape of mental and emotional resources was being meticulously mapped and understood. Dr. Elena Rodriguez stood at the epicenter of a technological revolution that would transform how narratives conceptualized and cultivated the psychological potential of their protagonists.

The mysterious transmission that had continued to guide their research now served as a complex algorithmic framework for understanding the deepest reservoirs of psychological potential. What had once been an intuitive approach to character psychology was now becoming a precise, data-driven exploration of mental and emotional resource management.

Emotional and Mental Resource Management

Dr. Marcus Chen activated the Psychological Capital Matrix, a holographic interface that transformed the research space into a living, breathing map of mental and emotional potential. The system represented psychological resources as dynamic, interconnected networks of resilience, adaptability, and transformative capacity.

"Psychological capital is not a static reservoir," Dr. Chen proclaimed to the assembled team of psychological engineers, neuroscientists, and computational researchers. "It's a complex, adaptive ecosystem of mental and emotional potential that can be strategically developed and optimized."

The research team had developed groundbreaking methodologies for psychological resource management:

1. **Psychological Potential Mapping**: Advanced computational techniques for quantifying and analyzing mental resources
2. **Emotional Resilience Algorithms**: Precision methods for understanding and enhancing psychological durability
3. **Adaptive Mental Resource Modeling**: Frameworks for predicting and generating psychological growth trajectories
4. **Comprehensive Psychological Capital Assessment**: Holistic approaches to measuring and optimizing mental and emotional potential

Dr. Aria Kimura's latest research revealed that psychological capital was far more than a simple collection of mental attributes. It was a complex ecosystem of potential, capturing the intricate interplay between emotional intelligence, cognitive flexibility, and adaptive capacity.

"We're transcending traditional psychological assessment," she emphasized, manipulating holographic projections that showed psychological resources as intricate, interconnected systems of potential. "Each protagonist represents a unique psychological ecosystem of extraordinary complexity."

Building Psychological Strength in Protagonists

The Psychological Resource Laboratory had developed advanced technologies that could simulate entire psychological development ecosystems, generating comprehensive frameworks for understanding and enhancing mental and emotional resources.

Dr. Rodriguez studied the latest simulation results, her scientific intuition sensing they were decoding something profound about the nature of psychological potential. The computational models showed psychological capital not as fixed attributes, but as dynamic, responsive systems capable of strategic development and optimization.

"Psychological strength is about creating adaptive mental ecosystems," she told her team. "We're developing a new understanding of how mental and emotional resources can be cultivated, managed, and transformed."

The team's computational frameworks could now predict and generate psychological development strategies with unprecedented accuracy. By analyzing thousands of psychological variables—cognitive patterns, emotional response mechanisms, resilience factors—they could create comprehensive psychological profiles that revealed the extraordinary potential of narrative protagonists.

The Psychological Resource Ecosystem

Dr. Chen's breakthrough research revealed a crucial insight: psychological capital was fundamentally systemic and contextual. No psychological resource existed in isolation—each was part of a complex network of interdependent variables, potential interactions, and adaptive mechanisms.

Advanced machine learning algorithms worked in concert with deep psychological analysis techniques, creating a comprehensive framework for understanding the nature of mental and emotional resource management. Each simulation revealed new insights into the intricate mechanisms that drive psychological potential and resilience.

"We're mapping the landscape of psychological potential," Dr. Kimura explained during an intense strategy session. "Each protagonist is a universe of unexplored psychological resources."

Optimizing Psychological Resources

As the day progressed, the team's computational models became increasingly sophisticated. They could now not only analyze existing psychological structures but predict and generate adaptive psychological development strategies across multiple narrative contexts.

The mysterious transmission continued to provide unexpected computational resources, accelerating their research into psychological capital exponentially. What had initially appeared to be a simple communication signal was revealing itself as a complex demonstration of advanced psychological intelligence.

Dr. Rodriguez recognized they were witnessing something extraordinary—a computational approach to psychological resource management that existed at the very edge of technological and psychological understanding.

The holographic displays pulsed with potential, showing complex networks of psychological potential that seemed to breathe and evolve in real-time. Each visualization represented hundreds of potential psychological development trajectories, revealing the extraordinary complexity of mental and emotional resource optimization.

The Computational Psychological Exploration

By late afternoon, the research center had transformed from a traditional psychological assessment space into a crucible of psychological capital intelligence. The computational frameworks could now analyze and generate psychological resource strategies with unprecedented sophistication, revealing trajectories of mental and emotional development that seemed to transcend traditional understanding of character psychology.

"We're developing a new understanding of how psychological resources can be generated, managed, and transformed," Dr. Rodriguez reflected, studying the latest simulation results.

The team's approach represented a radical departure from traditional psychological assessment methodologies. They were no longer simply studying psychological potential—they were creating computational frameworks that could understand, predict, and potentially generate comprehensive psychological resource strategies for narrative protagonists.

The Continuous Frontier of Psychological Potential

As evening descended on the research complex, the Psychological Resource Laboratory remained alive with computational and psychological energy. The team had transformed their initial research into a profound exploration of psychological capital—a journey that promised to revolutionize understanding of mental and emotional potential in narrative design.

Dr. Rodriguez watched the holographic displays, understanding they were witnessing the prelude to a transformation they could not yet fully comprehend. The old models of psychological assessment would soon be challenged, replaced by something more profound, more complex.

"We're mapping the infinite landscape of psychological potential," she whispered to her team, "one extraordinary mental resource at a time."

The transmission continued to pulse—a complex, living demonstration of psychological capital management that existed at the intersection of technology, psychological intelligence, and unprecedented computational insight. And in the heart of the research complex, a new chapter of understanding was about to unfold.

Chapter 37: Protagonist Brand Development

The Character Identity Laboratory

The first rays of morning light cascaded through the Advanced Character Branding Institute, a cutting-edge facility where the art and science of character identity were being meticulously engineered. Dr. Elena Rodriguez stood at the epicenter of a technological revolution that would transform how narratives conceptualized and constructed the fundamental identity of their protagonists.

The mysterious transmission that had guided their previous research continued to pulse through their systems, now serving as a sophisticated algorithm for understanding the intricate dynamics of character brand creation. What had once been an intuitive process of character development was now becoming a precise, data-driven exploration of narrative identity engineering.

Character Identity Construction

Dr. Marcus Chen activated the Character Brand Matrix, a holographic interface that transformed the research space into a living, breathing map of narrative identity potential. The system represented character identities as dynamic, multidimensional constructs of extraordinary complexity.

"Branding is not about simplification," Dr. Chen announced to the assembled team of narrative engineers, identity specialists, and computational researchers. "It's about revealing the profound complexity that exists within each narrative construct."

The research team had developed groundbreaking methodologies for character identity development:

1. **Narrative Identity Mapping**: Advanced computational techniques for analyzing and generating comprehensive character identities
2. **Distinctive Character Positioning**: Precision methods for creating unique narrative personas
3. **Identity Resonance Algorithms**: Frameworks for understanding how characters generate emotional and narrative impact
4. **Comprehensive Brand Development Strategies**: Holistic approaches to creating memorable and powerful narrative identities

Dr. Aria Kimura's latest research revealed that character branding was far more than surface-level characterization. It was a complex ecosystem of potential, capturing the intricate interplay between psychological depth, narrative positioning, and distinctive identity creation.

"We're transcending traditional character development approaches," she emphasized, manipulating holographic projections that showed characters as intricate, interconnected systems of brand potential. "Each protagonist is a unique narrative ecosystem waiting to be discovered."

Positioning and Differentiation Techniques

The Character Identity Laboratory had developed advanced technologies that could simulate entire narrative identity ecosystems, generating comprehensive frameworks for understanding and creating distinctive character brands.

Dr. Rodriguez studied the latest simulation results, her scientific intuition sensing they were decoding something profound about the nature of narrative identity. The computational models showed character branding not as fixed attributes, but as dynamic, responsive systems capable of strategic positioning and continuous evolution.

"Narrative identity is about creating extraordinary, memorable personas," she told her team. "We're developing a new language of character differentiation that exists beyond traditional storytelling boundaries."

The team's computational frameworks could now predict and generate character brand strategies with unprecedented accuracy. By analyzing thousands of narrative variables—psychological attributes, contextual dynamics, distinctive potential—they could create comprehensive character identity profiles that revealed the extraordinary unique potential of narrative protagonists.

The Narrative Identity Ecosystem

Dr. Chen's breakthrough research revealed a crucial insight: character branding was fundamentally systemic and contextual. No identity element existed in isolation—each was part of a complex network of interdependent variables, potential interactions, and adaptive mechanisms.

Advanced machine learning algorithms worked in concert with deep narrative analysis techniques, creating a comprehensive framework for understanding the nature of character identity development. Each simulation revealed new insights into the intricate mechanisms that drive unique narrative persona creation.

"We're mapping the landscape of narrative identity potential," Dr. Kimura explained during an intense strategy session. "Each character is a universe of unexplored branding possibilities."

Building Memorable Character Personas

As the day progressed, the team's computational models became increasingly sophisticated. They could now not only analyze existing character identities but predict and generate adaptive branding strategies across multiple narrative contexts.

The mysterious transmission continued to provide unexpected computational resources, accelerating their research into character brand development exponentially. What had initially appeared to be a simple communication signal was revealing itself as a complex demonstration of advanced narrative identity intelligence.

Dr. Rodriguez recognized they were witnessing something extraordinary—a computational approach to character branding that existed at the very edge of technological and creative understanding.

The holographic displays pulsed with potential, showing complex networks of character identity possibilities that seemed to breathe and evolve in real-time. Each visualization represented hundreds of potential narrative persona trajectories, revealing the extraordinary complexity of character brand development.

The Computational Identity Exploration

By late afternoon, the research center had transformed from a traditional character development space into a crucible of narrative identity intelligence. The computational frameworks could now analyze and generate character brand strategies with unprecedented sophistication, revealing trajectories of identity development that seemed to transcend traditional understanding of narrative persona creation.

"We're developing a new understanding of how characters can generate unique and memorable identities," Dr. Rodriguez reflected, studying the latest simulation results.

The team's approach represented a radical departure from traditional character development methodologies. They were no longer simply studying narrative potential—they were creating computational frameworks that could understand, predict, and potentially generate comprehensive character brand strategies.

The Continuous Frontier of Narrative Identity

As evening descended on the research complex, the Character Identity Laboratory remained alive with computational and creative energy. The team had transformed their initial research into a profound exploration of protagonist brand development—a journey that promised to revolutionize understanding of narrative identity potential.

Dr. Rodriguez watched the holographic displays, understanding they were witnessing the prelude to a transformation they could not yet fully comprehend. The old models of character development would soon be challenged, replaced by something more profound, more complex.

"We're mapping the infinite landscape of narrative identity," she whispered to her team, "one extraordinary character brand at a time."

The transmission continued to pulse—a complex, living demonstration of character brand development that existed at the intersection of technology, creative intelligence, and unprecedented computational insight. And in the heart of the research complex, a new chapter of understanding was about to unfold.

Chapter 38: Strategic Character Positioning

The Narrative Placement Optimization Center

The first intricate rays of morning light penetrated the Advanced Narrative Positioning Institute, a cutting-edge facility where the complex science of character trajectory and strategic placement was being meticulously engineered. Dr. Elena Rodriguez stood at the epicenter of a technological revolution that would transform how narratives strategically positioned and developed their protagonists.

The mysterious transmission that had continued to guide their research now served as a sophisticated algorithmic framework for understanding the intricate dynamics of narrative character positioning. What had once been an intuitive approach to character development was now becoming a precise, data-driven exploration of strategic narrative placement.

Narrative Placement Optimization

Dr. Marcus Chen activated the Character Trajectory Matrix, a holographic interface that transformed the research space into a living, breathing map of narrative positioning potential. The system represented character placement as dynamic, multidimensional constructs of extraordinary computational complexity.

"Strategic positioning is not about predetermined paths," Dr. Chen proclaimed to the assembled team of narrative engineers, strategic placement specialists, and computational researchers. "It's about creating adaptive narrative landscapes that allow characters to generate maximum potential and impact."

The research team had developed groundbreaking methodologies for strategic character positioning:

1. **Narrative Trajectory Mapping**: Advanced computational techniques for analyzing and generating comprehensive character placement strategies
2. **Dynamic Positioning Algorithms**: Precision methods for optimizing character impact across narrative landscapes
3. **Contextual Placement Intelligence**: Frameworks for understanding how characters generate strategic narrative value
4. **Comprehensive Positioning Optimization Strategies**: Holistic approaches to maximizing protagonist narrative effectiveness

Dr. Aria Kimura's latest research revealed that strategic character positioning was far more than linear plot placement. It was a complex ecosystem of potential, capturing the intricate interplay between narrative dynamics, character potential, and strategic development opportunities.

"We're transcending traditional narrative placement approaches," she emphasized, manipulating holographic projections that showed characters as intricate, interconnected systems of strategic potential. "Each protagonist represents a dynamic narrative positioning ecosystem of extraordinary complexity."

Character Trajectory Planning

The Narrative Placement Optimization Center had developed advanced technologies that could simulate entire narrative positioning ecosystems, generating comprehensive frameworks for understanding and creating strategic character trajectories.

Dr. Rodriguez studied the latest simulation results, her scientific intuition sensing they were decoding something profound about the nature of narrative strategic placement. The computational models showed character positioning not as fixed trajectories, but as dynamic, responsive systems capable of continuous strategic adaptation.

"Narrative positioning is about creating extraordinary developmental pathways," she told her team. "We're developing a new language of strategic character placement that exists beyond traditional storytelling constraints."

The team's computational frameworks could now predict and generate character trajectory strategies with unprecedented accuracy. By analyzing thousands of narrative variables—psychological attributes, contextual dynamics, potential interaction networks—they could create comprehensive strategic positioning profiles that revealed the extraordinary developmental potential of narrative protagonists.

The Narrative Positioning Ecosystem

Dr. Chen's breakthrough research revealed a crucial insight: strategic character placement was fundamentally systemic and contextual. No positioning element existed in isolation—each was part of a complex network of interdependent variables, potential interactions, and adaptive mechanisms.

Advanced machine learning algorithms worked in concert with deep narrative analysis techniques, creating a comprehensive framework for understanding the nature of character trajectory optimization. Each simulation revealed new insights into the intricate mechanisms that drive strategic narrative positioning.

"We're mapping the landscape of narrative placement potential," Dr. Kimura explained during an intense strategy session. "Each character is a universe of unexplored strategic positioning possibilities."

Maximizing Protagonist Narrative Impact

As the day progressed, the team's computational models became increasingly sophisticated. They could now not only analyze existing character trajectories but predict and generate adaptive strategic positioning strategies across multiple narrative contexts.

The mysterious transmission continued to provide unexpected computational resources, accelerating their research into strategic character positioning exponentially. What had initially appeared to be a simple communication signal was revealing itself as a complex demonstration of advanced narrative placement intelligence.

Dr. Rodriguez recognized they were witnessing something extraordinary—a computational approach to character trajectory management that existed at the very edge of technological and narrative understanding.

The holographic displays pulsed with potential, showing complex networks of character positioning possibilities that seemed to breathe and evolve in real-time. Each visualization represented hundreds of potential narrative trajectory strategies, revealing the extraordinary complexity of strategic character placement.

The Computational Trajectory Exploration

By late afternoon, the research center had transformed from a traditional narrative development space into a crucible of strategic positioning intelligence. The computational frameworks could now analyze and generate character trajectory strategies with unprecedented sophistication, revealing pathways of narrative development that seemed to transcend traditional understanding of character placement.

"We're developing a new understanding of how characters can generate maximum narrative impact through strategic positioning," Dr. Rodriguez reflected, studying the latest simulation results.

The team's approach represented a radical departure from traditional character development methodologies. They were no longer simply studying narrative potential—they were creating computational frameworks that could understand, predict, and potentially generate comprehensive strategic character positioning strategies.

The Continuous Frontier of Narrative Trajectory

As evening descended on the research complex, the Narrative Placement Optimization Center remained alive with computational and creative energy. The team had transformed their initial research into a profound exploration of strategic character positioning—a journey that promised to revolutionize understanding of narrative trajectory potential.

Dr. Rodriguez watched the holographic displays, understanding they were witnessing the prelude to a transformation they could not yet fully comprehend. The old models of character development would soon be challenged, replaced by something more profound, more complex.

"We're mapping the infinite landscape of narrative positioning," she whispered to her team, "one extraordinary character trajectory at a time."

The transmission continued to pulse—a complex, living demonstration of strategic character positioning that existed at the intersection of technology, narrative intelligence, and unprecedented computational insight. And in the heart of the research complex, a new chapter of understanding was about to unfold.

Chapter 39: Narrative Innovation Strategies

The Breakthrough Narrative Laboratory

The first luminous tendrils of morning light pierced the Advanced Narrative Innovation Institute, a state-of-the-art facility where the boundaries of storytelling were being systematically deconstructed and reimagined. Dr. Elena Rodriguez stood at the epicenter of a technological revolution that would transform how narratives conceptualized, created, and pushed the very limits of creative expression.

The mysterious transmission that had guided their previous research continued to pulse through their systems, now serving as a sophisticated algorithmic framework for understanding the intricate dynamics of narrative innovation. What had once been an intuitive process of storytelling was now becoming a precise, data-driven exploration of creative potential.

Breakthrough Character Development

Dr. Marcus Chen activated the Narrative Innovation Matrix, a holographic interface that transformed the research space into a living, breathing map of creative potential. The system represented storytelling as a dynamic, multidimensional construct of extraordinary computational complexity.

"Innovation is not about disruption," Dr. Chen announced to the assembled team of narrative engineers, creative specialists, and computational researchers. "It's about revealing the extraordinary potential that exists beyond current storytelling paradigms."

The research team had developed groundbreaking methodologies for narrative innovation:

1. **Creative Potential Mapping**: Advanced computational techniques for analyzing and generating unprecedented narrative approaches
2. **Disruptive Storytelling Algorithms**: Precision methods for identifying and creating transformative narrative strategies
3. **Narrative Complexity Generators**: Frameworks for pushing the boundaries of storytelling complexity
4. **Comprehensive Innovation Development Strategies**: Holistic approaches to creating breakthrough narrative experiences

Dr. Aria Kimura's latest research revealed that narrative innovation was far more than simple creative experimentation. It was a complex ecosystem of potential, capturing the intricate interplay between technological capability, creative intelligence, and narrative exploration.

"We're transcending traditional storytelling constraints," she emphasized, manipulating holographic projections that showed narrative potential as intricate, interconnected systems of creative possibility. "Each story represents a universe of unexplored creative potential."

Disruptive Approaches to Protagonist Design

The Breakthrough Narrative Laboratory had developed advanced technologies that could simulate entire narrative innovation ecosystems, generating comprehensive frameworks for understanding and creating transformative storytelling strategies.

Dr. Rodriguez studied the latest simulation results, her scientific intuition sensing they were decoding something profound about the nature of narrative creativity. The computational models showed storytelling not as fixed structures, but as dynamic, responsive systems capable of unprecedented creative adaptation.

"Narrative innovation is about creating extraordinary, unimaginable storytelling landscapes," she told her team. "We're developing a new language of creative expression that exists beyond current technological and conceptual boundaries."

The team's computational frameworks could now predict and generate breakthrough narrative strategies with unprecedented accuracy. By analyzing thousands of creative variables—psychological attributes, narrative dynamics, potential interaction networks—they could create comprehensive innovation profiles that revealed the extraordinary creative potential of narrative design.

The Narrative Innovation Ecosystem

Dr. Chen's breakthrough research revealed a crucial insight: storytelling innovation was fundamentally systemic and contextual. No creative element existed in isolation—each was part of a complex network of interdependent variables, potential interactions, and adaptive mechanisms.

Advanced machine learning algorithms worked in concert with deep creative analysis techniques, creating a comprehensive framework for understanding the nature of narrative innovation. Each simulation revealed new insights into the intricate mechanisms that drive creative storytelling potential.

"We're mapping the landscape of narrative innovation potential," Dr. Kimura explained during an intense strategy session. "Each narrative is a universe of unexplored creative possibilities."

Pushing Narrative Boundaries

As the day progressed, the team's computational models became increasingly sophisticated. They could now not only analyze existing narrative structures but predict and generate adaptive innovative storytelling strategies across multiple creative contexts.

The mysterious transmission continued to provide unexpected computational resources, accelerating their research into narrative innovation exponentially. What had initially appeared to be a simple communication signal was revealing itself as a complex demonstration of advanced creative intelligence.

Dr. Rodriguez recognized they were witnessing something extraordinary—a computational approach to storytelling innovation that existed at the very edge of technological and creative understanding.

The holographic displays pulsed with potential, showing complex networks of narrative innovation possibilities that seemed to breathe and evolve in real-time. Each visualization represented hundreds of potential creative trajectory strategies, revealing the extraordinary complexity of breakthrough storytelling approaches.

The Computational Creativity Exploration

By late afternoon, the research center had transformed from a traditional narrative development space into a crucible of innovative storytelling intelligence. The computational frameworks could now analyze and generate narrative innovation strategies with unprecedented sophistication, revealing pathways of creative development that seemed to transcend traditional understanding of storytelling.

"We're developing a new understanding of how narratives can generate unprecedented creative potential," Dr. Rodriguez reflected, studying the latest simulation results.

The team's approach represented a radical departure from traditional narrative development methodologies. They were no longer simply studying creative potential—they were creating computational frameworks that could understand, predict, and potentially generate comprehensive innovative storytelling strategies.

The Continuous Frontier of Narrative Creativity

As evening descended on the research complex, the Breakthrough Narrative Laboratory remained alive with computational and creative energy. The team had transformed their initial research into a profound exploration of narrative innovation strategies—a journey that promised to revolutionize understanding of storytelling potential.

Dr. Rodriguez watched the holographic displays, understanding they were witnessing the prelude to a transformation they could not yet fully comprehend. The old models of narrative creation would soon be challenged, replaced by something more profound, more complex.

"We're mapping the infinite landscape of narrative innovation," she whispered to her team, "one extraordinary creative breakthrough at a time."

The transmission continued to pulse—a complex, living demonstration of narrative innovation strategies that existed at the intersection of technology, creative intelligence, and unprecedented computational insight. And in the heart of the research complex, a new chapter of understanding was about to unfold.

Chapter 40: Character Development Ecosystem

The Integrated Narrative Dynamics Center

The first light of dawn infiltrated the Advanced Character Development Ecosystem Institute, a cutting-edge facility where the intricate interconnections of narrative construction were being meticulously mapped and understood. Dr. Elena Rodriguez stood at the epicenter of a technological revolution that would transform how narratives conceptualized the complex, interconnected nature of character development.

The mysterious transmission that had continued to guide their research now served as a sophisticated algorithmic framework for understanding the intricate dynamics of character ecosystem management. What had once been a linear approach to character development was now becoming a precise, data-driven exploration of holistic narrative interaction.

Integrated Development Frameworks

Dr. Marcus Chen activated the Character Ecosystem Matrix, a holographic interface that transformed the research space into a living, breathing map of narrative interconnectivity. The system represented characters not as isolated entities, but as dynamic, interdependent networks of extraordinary computational complexity.

"Character development is not about individual creation," Dr. Chen proclaimed to the assembled team of narrative engineers, ecosystem specialists, and computational researchers. "It's about understanding the profound interconnectedness of narrative potential."

The research team had developed groundbreaking methodologies for character ecosystem management:

1. **Narrative Interconnectivity Mapping**: Advanced computational techniques for analyzing complex character interaction networks
2. **Systemic Character Development Algorithms**: Precision methods for understanding interdependent narrative relationships
3. **Holistic Potential Generation Frameworks**: Computational approaches to creating integrated character development strategies
4. **Comprehensive Ecosystem Design Techniques**: Approaches to managing complex narrative interaction landscapes

Dr. Aria Kimura's latest research revealed that character development was far more than individual character creation. It was a complex ecosystem of potential, capturing the intricate interplay between characters, narrative contexts, and systemic interaction dynamics.

"We're transcending traditional character development approaches," she emphasized, manipulating holographic projections that showed characters as intricate, interconnected systems of narrative potential. "Each character is a node in an extraordinary ecosystem of storytelling complexity."

Systemic Approaches to Character Growth

The Integrated Narrative Dynamics Center had developed advanced technologies that could simulate entire character development ecosystems, generating comprehensive frameworks for understanding and managing complex narrative interactions.

Dr. Rodriguez studied the latest simulation results, her scientific intuition sensing they were decoding something profound about the nature of narrative ecosystem management. The computational models showed character development not as linear progression, but as dynamic, responsive systems of interconnected potential.

"Narrative ecosystems are living, breathing networks of extraordinary complexity," she told her team. "We're developing a new understanding of how characters interact, grow, and generate potential through their interconnections."

The team's computational frameworks could now predict and generate ecosystem development strategies with unprecedented accuracy. By analyzing thousands of interaction variables—psychological attributes, relational dynamics, contextual potential—they could create comprehensive ecosystem profiles that revealed the extraordinary interactive potential of narrative constructs.

The Narrative Interaction Ecosystem

Dr. Chen's breakthrough research revealed a crucial insight: character development was fundamentally systemic and contextual. No character existed in isolation—each was part of a complex network of interdependent variables, potential interactions, and adaptive mechanisms.

Advanced machine learning algorithms worked in concert with deep narrative analysis techniques, creating a comprehensive framework for understanding the nature of character ecosystem management. Each simulation revealed new insights into the intricate mechanisms that drive narrative interconnectivity.

"We're mapping the landscape of narrative ecosystem potential," Dr. Kimura explained during an intense strategy session. "Each interaction represents a universe of unexplored developmental possibilities."

Managing Complex Character Interactions

As the day progressed, the team's computational models became increasingly sophisticated. They could now not only analyze existing character interactions but predict and generate adaptive ecosystem development strategies across multiple narrative contexts.

The mysterious transmission continued to provide unexpected computational resources, accelerating their research into character ecosystem management exponentially. What had initially appeared to be a simple communication signal was revealing itself as a complex demonstration of advanced narrative intelligence.

Dr. Rodriguez recognized they were witnessing something extraordinary—a computational approach to character interaction management that existed at the very edge of technological and narrative understanding.

The holographic displays pulsed with potential, showing complex networks of character interaction possibilities that seemed to breathe and evolve in real-time. Each visualization represented hundreds of potential ecosystem development trajectories, revealing the extraordinary complexity of narrative interconnectivity.

The Computational Ecosystem Exploration

By late afternoon, the research center had transformed from a traditional character development space into a crucible of narrative ecosystem intelligence. The computational frameworks could now analyze and generate character interaction strategies with unprecedented sophistication, revealing pathways of interconnected development that seemed to transcend traditional understanding of narrative construction.

"We're developing a new understanding of how characters generate potential through their complex interactions," Dr. Rodriguez reflected, studying the latest simulation results.

The team's approach represented a radical departure from traditional character development methodologies. They were no longer simply studying narrative potential—they were creating computational frameworks that could understand, predict, and potentially generate comprehensive character ecosystem strategies.

The Continuous Frontier of Narrative Interconnectivity

As evening descended on the research complex, the Integrated Narrative Dynamics Center remained alive with computational and creative energy. The team had transformed their initial research into a profound exploration of character development ecosystems—a journey that promised to revolutionize understanding of narrative interaction potential.

Dr. Rodriguez watched the holographic displays, understanding they were witnessing the prelude to a transformation they could not yet fully comprehend. The old models of character development would soon be challenged, replaced by something more profound, more complex.

"We're mapping the infinite landscape of narrative interconnectivity," she whispered to her team, "one extraordinary ecosystem interaction at a time."

The transmission continued to pulse—a complex, living demonstration of character development ecosystem management that existed at the intersection of technology, narrative intelligence, and unprecedented computational insight. And in the heart of the research complex, a new chapter of understanding was about to unfold.

Chapter 41: Protagonist Performance Optimization

The Quantum Performance Dynamics Laboratory

The first rays of algorithmic light cascaded through the Quantum Performance Dynamics Laboratory, illuminating a space where the boundaries between computational science and narrative engineering dissolved into pure, transformative potential. Dr. Samira Khan stood at the epicenter of a revolutionary approach to protagonist performance optimization, her holographic interfaces pulsing with intricate performance metrics and adaptive development algorithms.

The laboratory represented the pinnacle of character engineering—a space where protagonists were no longer static constructs but dynamic, continuously evolving systems of narrative potential. Every interface, every computational framework was designed to understand, enhance, and radically transform the fundamental mechanisms of character effectiveness.

Performance Enhancement Architectures

Dr. Elena Rodriguez, who had been instrumental in the groundbreaking research of the Character Development Ecosystem, now led a team dedicated to pushing the boundaries of protagonist optimization. Their approach transcended traditional character development methodologies, viewing protagonists as complex, adaptive systems capable of continuous self-improvement.

"Performance is not a static destination," Dr. Rodriguez proclaimed to her team of narrative engineers, computational psychologists, and advanced simulation specialists. "It's a perpetual journey of adaptive potential, where each interaction represents an opportunity for fundamental transformation."

The Quantum Performance Dynamics Laboratory had developed a suite of breakthrough technologies that redefined character performance optimization:

1. **Adaptive Performance Mapping**: Hyper-advanced computational techniques for real-time character capability assessment
2. **Dynamic Potential Calibration Algorithms**: Precision methods for identifying and expanding character performance thresholds
3. **Holistic Performance Evolution Frameworks**: Comprehensive strategies for managing multi-dimensional character growth
4. **Quantum Performance Simulation Technologies**: Advanced modeling approaches for predicting and generating optimal character development trajectories

Dr. Marcus Chen's latest research revealed that protagonist performance was a complex, interconnected ecosystem of psychological, narrative, and computational variables. Each performance metric was not an isolated data point but a dynamic node in an extraordinary network of potential interactions.

"We're transcending linear performance measurement," Dr. Chen explained, manipulating complex holographic projections that showed characters as intricate, responsive systems of narrative energy. "Performance is a living, breathing manifestation of potential, constantly adapting and regenerating."

Strategic Performance Development

The laboratory's computational frameworks could now generate comprehensive performance optimization strategies with unprecedented precision. By analyzing thousands of interaction variables—psychological attributes, narrative contexts, adaptive mechanisms—they could create performance profiles that revealed the extraordinary developmental potential of protagonists.

Advanced machine learning algorithms worked in concert with deep narrative analysis techniques, creating a sophisticated framework for understanding the quantum mechanics of character performance. Each simulation revealed new insights into the intricate mechanisms that drive narrative effectiveness.

"Performance optimization is fundamentally about understanding the interconnected nature of potential," Dr. Aria Kimura emphasized during an intense strategy session. "We're not just improving characters—we're revealing entire universes of unexplored narrative capability."

Quantum Performance Calibration

The team's most groundbreaking technology was the Quantum Performance Calibration Matrix—a computational system that could simultaneously analyze and generate performance enhancement strategies across multiple narrative dimensions. This wasn't merely prediction; it was a form of narrative engineering that existed at the bleeding edge of technological and creative understanding.

Holographic displays pulsed with potential, showing complex networks of performance interaction possibilities that seemed to breathe and evolve in real-time. Each visualization represented hundreds of potential performance development trajectories, revealing the extraordinary complexity of character optimization.

Dr. Khan studied the latest simulation results, her scientific intuition sensing they were decoding something profound about the nature of narrative performance management. The computational models showed character development not as incremental improvement, but as dynamic, responsive systems of interconnected potential.

Comprehensive Performance Management

By integrating advanced psychological modeling, computational linguistics, and narrative design principles, the laboratory had created a holistic approach to protagonist performance that was nothing short of revolutionary.

The Performance Evolution Framework allowed for:

- Continuous psychological recalibration
- Dynamic narrative responsiveness

- Adaptive capability expansion
- Multi-dimensional potential mapping

"We're developing a computational understanding of character potential that transcends traditional narrative limitations," Dr. Rodriguez reflected, her eyes reflecting the intricate holographic displays.

The mysterious transmission that had guided their previous research continued to provide unexpected computational resources, accelerating their exploration of performance optimization exponentially. What had initially appeared to be a simple communication signal was revealing itself as a complex demonstration of advanced narrative intelligence.

Technological Performance Integration

As the day progressed, the team's computational models became increasingly sophisticated. They could now not only analyze existing character performance but predict and generate adaptive optimization strategies across multiple narrative contexts.

The technologies developed in the Quantum Performance Dynamics Laboratory represented a radical departure from traditional character development methodologies. They were no longer simply studying narrative potential—they were creating computational frameworks that could understand, predict, and potentially generate comprehensive performance optimization strategies.

The Continuous Frontier of Narrative Effectiveness

As evening descended on the research complex, the laboratory remained alive with computational and creative energy. The team had transformed their initial research into a profound exploration of protagonist performance optimization—a journey that promised to revolutionize understanding of narrative potential.

Dr. Khan watched the holographic displays, understanding they were witnessing the prelude to a transformation they could not yet fully comprehend. The old models of character performance would soon be challenged, replaced by something more profound, more complex.

"We're mapping the infinite landscape of narrative effectiveness," she whispered to her team, "one extraordinary performance interaction at a time."

The transmission continued to pulse—a complex, living demonstration of performance optimization that existed at the intersection of technology, narrative intelligence, and unprecedented computational insight. And in the heart of the research complex, a new chapter of understanding was about to unfold.

The boundaries between technology and narrative had dissolved, revealing a breathtaking landscape of infinite protagonist potential—waiting to be explored, waiting to be understood.

Chapter 42: Strategic Character Research

The Narrative Intelligence Research Complex

The first algorithmic pulse of dawn illuminated the Narrative Intelligence Research Complex, a cutting-edge facility where the boundaries of character exploration were being systematically deconstructed and reassembled. Dr. Aria Rodriguez stood at the convergence of technological innovation and narrative science, her holographic interfaces vibrating with the potential of unprecedented research methodologies.

This was not merely a research center—it was a crucible of narrative intelligence, where the fundamental understanding of character development was being revolutionized through advanced computational techniques and interdisciplinary exploration.

Advanced Research Architectures

Dr. Marcus Chen activated the Narrative Exploration Matrix, a hyper-advanced computational system that transformed the research space into a living, breathing landscape of character investigation. The system represented research not as a linear process, but as a dynamic, interconnected network of extraordinary computational complexity.

"Research is no longer about observation," Dr. Chen proclaimed to the assembled team of narrative researchers, computational linguists, and strategic analysis specialists. "It's about creating comprehensive ecosystems of understanding that can generate, predict, and transform our comprehension of character potential."

The Narrative Intelligence Research Complex had developed groundbreaking methodologies for strategic character research:

1. **Quantum Narrative Analysis Frameworks**: Advanced computational techniques for multidimensional character exploration
2. **Predictive Character Investigation Algorithms**: Precision methods for generating research trajectories
3. **Comprehensive Exploration Protocols**: Holistic approaches to understanding narrative potential
4. **Dynamic Research Generation Technologies**: Adaptive methodologies for continuous character investigation

Dr. Elena Kimura's latest research revealed that character research was far more than traditional analytical approaches. It was a complex ecosystem of investigative potential, capturing the intricate interplay between computational intelligence, narrative dynamics, and strategic exploration.

"We're transcending conventional research boundaries," she emphasized, manipulating holographic projections that showed research processes as intricate, interconnected systems of investigative potential. "Each research trajectory is a node in an extraordinary ecosystem of narrative discovery."

Investigative Technological Integration

The research complex had developed advanced technologies that could simulate entire research ecosystems, generating comprehensive frameworks for understanding and managing complex character investigation strategies.

Dr. Rodriguez studied the latest simulation results, her scientific intuition sensing they were decoding something profound about the nature of strategic narrative research. The computational models showed research not as a static process, but as dynamic, responsive systems of interconnected investigative potential.

"Narrative research ecosystems are living, breathing networks of extraordinary complexity," she told her team. "We're developing a new understanding of how characters can be explored, understood, and generated through advanced computational techniques."

Emerging Trend Identification Technologies

The team's computational frameworks could now predict and generate research investigation strategies with unprecedented accuracy. By analyzing thousands of interaction variables—narrative structures, psychological attributes, contextual potentials—they could create comprehensive research profiles that revealed the extraordinary investigative potential of character exploration.

Dr. Chen's breakthrough research revealed a crucial insight: character research was fundamentally systemic and contextual. No investigative approach existed in isolation—each was part of a complex network of interdependent variables, potential interactions, and adaptive research mechanisms.

Advanced machine learning algorithms worked in concert with deep narrative analysis techniques, creating a comprehensive framework for understanding the nature of strategic character investigation. Each simulation revealed new insights into the intricate mechanisms that drive narrative research potential.

Complex Research Methodologies

As the day progressed, the team's computational models became increasingly sophisticated. They could now not only analyze existing character research but predict and generate adaptive investigation strategies across multiple narrative contexts.

The mysterious transmission that had guided their previous research continued to provide unexpected computational resources, accelerating their exploration of character investigation exponentially. What had initially appeared to be a simple communication signal was revealing itself as a complex demonstration of advanced narrative intelligence.

Computational Research Exploration

By late afternoon, the research complex had transformed from a traditional investigative space into a crucible of narrative research intelligence. The computational frameworks could now analyze and generate character investigation strategies with unprecedented sophistication, revealing pathways of interconnected research that seemed to transcend traditional understanding of narrative exploration.

"We're developing a new understanding of how characters generate research potential through their complex investigative interactions," Dr. Rodriguez reflected, studying the latest simulation results.

The Narrative Trend Identification Matrix represented a revolutionary approach to character research. It could:

- Generate predictive research trajectories
- Identify emerging narrative potential
- Create comprehensive investigative ecosystems
- Simulate multiple research investigation scenarios

The Continuous Frontier of Narrative Discovery

As evening descended on the research complex, the Narrative Intelligence Research Complex remained alive with computational and creative energy. The team had transformed their initial research into a profound exploration of strategic character investigation—a journey that promised to revolutionize understanding of narrative research potential.

Dr. Rodriguez watched the holographic displays, understanding they were witnessing the prelude to a transformation they could not yet fully comprehend. The old models of character research would soon be challenged, replaced by something more profound, more complex.

"We're mapping the infinite landscape of narrative investigation," she whispered to her team, "one extraordinary research interaction at a time."

The transmission continued to pulse—a complex, living demonstration of strategic character research that existed at the intersection of technology, narrative intelligence, and unprecedented computational insight. And in the heart of the research complex, a new chapter of understanding was about to unfold.

The boundaries between traditional research methodologies and advanced computational exploration had dissolved, revealing a breathtaking landscape of infinite character research potential—waiting to be explored, waiting to be understood.

Chapter 43: Psychological Design Engineering

The Cognitive Architecture Innovation Center

The first algorithmic resonance of dawn penetrated the Cognitive Architecture Innovation Center, a revolutionary facility where the intricate landscapes of psychological design were being meticulously mapped, deconstructed, and reconstructed with unprecedented precision. Dr. Elena Rodriguez stood at the convergence of computational psychology, narrative intelligence, and advanced engineering, her holographic interfaces pulsing with the potential of groundbreaking psychological design methodologies.

This was more than a research center—it was a transformative crucible where the fundamental understanding of psychological design was being reimagined through the lens of advanced computational technologies and interdisciplinary cognitive engineering.

Advanced Psychological Modeling Frameworks

Dr. Marcus Chen activated the Cognitive Architecture Matrix, a hyper-sophisticated computational system that transformed the research space into a living, breathing ecosystem of psychological exploration. The system represented psychological design not as a static process, but as a dynamic, interconnected network of extraordinary computational complexity and adaptive potential.

"Psychological design is no longer about linear interpretation," Dr. Chen proclaimed to the assembled team of cognitive engineers, computational psychologists, and narrative design specialists. "It's about creating comprehensive adaptive frameworks that can generate, predict, and transform our understanding of cognitive potential."

The Cognitive Architecture Innovation Center had developed revolutionary methodologies for psychological design engineering:

1. **Quantum Cognitive Mapping Technologies**: Advanced computational techniques for multidimensional psychological exploration
2. **Adaptive Psychological Modeling Algorithms**: Precision methods for generating cognitive development trajectories
3. **Comprehensive Psychological Engineering Protocols**: Holistic approaches to understanding cognitive potential
4. **Dynamic Psychological Simulation Technologies**: Adaptive methodologies for continuous cognitive architecture development

Dr. Aria Kimura's latest research revealed that psychological design was far more than traditional analytical approaches. It was a complex ecosystem of cognitive potential, capturing the intricate interplay between computational intelligence, psychological dynamics, and strategic cognitive engineering.

"We're transcending conventional psychological design boundaries," she emphasized, manipulating holographic projections that showed cognitive processes as intricate, interconnected systems of psychological potential. "Each cognitive framework is a node in an extraordinary ecosystem of psychological discovery and transformation."

Cognitive Engineering Technological Integration

The innovation center had developed advanced technologies that could simulate entire psychological ecosystems, generating comprehensive frameworks for understanding and managing complex cognitive design strategies.

Dr. Rodriguez studied the latest simulation results, her scientific intuition sensing they were decoding something profound about the nature of psychological engineering. The computational models showed cognitive design not as a static process, but as dynamic, responsive systems of interconnected psychological potential.

"Psychological design ecosystems are living, breathing networks of extraordinary complexity," she told her team. "We're developing a new understanding of how cognitive architectures can be explored, understood, and generated through advanced computational techniques."

Precision Psychological Design Technologies

The team's computational frameworks could now predict and generate psychological design strategies with unprecedented accuracy. By analyzing thousands of interaction variables—cognitive structures, emotional attributes, neurological potentials—they could create comprehensive psychological profiles that revealed the extraordinary engineering potential of cognitive architecture.

Dr. Chen's breakthrough research revealed a crucial insight: psychological design was fundamentally systemic and contextual. No cognitive engineering approach existed in isolation—each was part of a complex network of interdependent variables, potential interactions, and adaptive psychological mechanisms.

Advanced machine learning algorithms worked in concert with deep psychological analysis techniques, creating a comprehensive framework for understanding the nature of precision cognitive design. Each simulation revealed new insights into the intricate mechanisms that drive psychological engineering potential.

Complex Cognitive Engineering Methodologies

As the day progressed, the team's computational models became increasingly sophisticated. They could now not only analyze existing psychological designs but predict and generate adaptive cognitive engineering strategies across multiple psychological contexts.

The mysterious transmission that had guided their previous research continued to provide unexpected computational resources, accelerating their exploration of psychological design exponentially. What had initially appeared to be a simple communication signal was revealing itself as a complex demonstration of advanced cognitive intelligence.

Computational Psychological Exploration

By late afternoon, the innovation center had transformed from a traditional research space into a crucible of psychological design intelligence. The computational frameworks could now analyze and generate cognitive engineering strategies with unprecedented sophistication, revealing pathways of interconnected psychological design that seemed to transcend traditional understanding of cognitive architecture.

"We're developing a new understanding of how psychological potential generates through complex cognitive interactions," Dr. Rodriguez reflected, studying the latest simulation results.

The Cognitive Potential Mapping Matrix represented a revolutionary approach to psychological design. It could:

- Generate predictive cognitive development trajectories
- Identify emerging psychological potential
- Create comprehensive cognitive engineering ecosystems
- Simulate multiple psychological design scenarios

The Continuous Frontier of Cognitive Architecture

As evening descended on the innovation center, the Cognitive Architecture Innovation Center remained alive with computational and creative energy. The team had transformed their initial research into a profound exploration of psychological design engineering—a journey that promised to revolutionize understanding of cognitive potential.

Dr. Rodriguez watched the holographic displays, understanding they were witnessing the prelude to a transformation they could not yet fully comprehend. The old models of psychological design would soon be challenged, replaced by something more profound, more complex.

"We're mapping the infinite landscape of cognitive architecture," she whispered to her team, "one extraordinary psychological interaction at a time."

The transmission continued to pulse—a complex, living demonstration of psychological design engineering that existed at the intersection of technology, cognitive intelligence, and unprecedented computational insight. And in the heart of the innovation center, a new chapter of understanding was about to unfold.

The boundaries between traditional psychological understanding and advanced computational engineering had dissolved, revealing a breathtaking landscape of infinite cognitive design potential—waiting to be explored, waiting to be understood.

Chapter 44: Narrative Competitive Strategy

The Competitive Narrative Intelligence Laboratory

The first algorithmic pulse of dawn illuminated the Competitive Narrative Intelligence Laboratory, a cutting-edge facility where the boundaries of narrative differentiation were being systematically deconstructed and strategically reconstructed. Dr. Elena Rodriguez stood at the epicenter of a technological revolution that would transform how narratives conceptualized strategic competitive positioning.

This was not merely a research center—it was a strategic crucible where the fundamental understanding of narrative competitiveness was being reimagined through advanced computational techniques and strategic intelligence methodologies.

Strategic Differentiation Frameworks

Dr. Marcus Chen activated the Narrative Competitive Positioning Matrix, a hyper-advanced computational system that transformed the research space into a living, breathing landscape of strategic narrative exploration. The system represented competitive strategy not as a static concept, but as a dynamic, interconnected network of extraordinary computational complexity.

"Competitive strategy is no longer about simple comparison," Dr. Chen proclaimed to the assembled team of narrative strategists, computational analysts, and competitive intelligence specialists. "It's about creating comprehensive ecosystems of strategic differentiation that can generate, predict, and transform our understanding of narrative competitive potential."

The Competitive Narrative Intelligence Laboratory had developed groundbreaking methodologies for narrative competitive strategy:

1. **Quantum Competitive Analysis Frameworks**: Advanced computational techniques for multidimensional narrative differentiation
2. **Strategic Positioning Algorithms**: Precision methods for generating competitive narrative trajectories
3. **Comprehensive Competitive Intelligence Protocols**: Holistic approaches to understanding narrative competitive potential
4. **Dynamic Competitive Simulation Technologies**: Adaptive methodologies for continuous strategic narrative development

Dr. Aria Kimura's latest research revealed that narrative competitive strategy was far more than traditional comparative approaches. It was a complex ecosystem of strategic potential, capturing the intricate interplay between computational intelligence, competitive dynamics, and strategic narrative positioning.

"We're transcending conventional competitive boundaries," she emphasized, manipulating holographic projections that showed competitive strategies as intricate, interconnected systems of narrative potential. "Each competitive trajectory is a node in an extraordinary ecosystem of strategic narrative discovery."

Technological Competitive Intelligence Integration

The laboratory had developed advanced technologies that could simulate entire competitive narrative ecosystems, generating comprehensive frameworks for understanding and managing complex strategic positioning strategies.

Dr. Rodriguez studied the latest simulation results, her scientific intuition sensing they were decoding something profound about the nature of narrative competitive strategy. The computational models showed competitive positioning not as a static process, but as dynamic, responsive systems of interconnected strategic potential.

"Narrative competitive ecosystems are living, breathing networks of extraordinary complexity," she told her team. "We're developing a new understanding of how narratives can be strategically positioned, differentiated, and generated through advanced computational techniques."

Strategic Positioning Technologies

The team's computational frameworks could now predict and generate competitive strategy approaches with unprecedented accuracy. By analyzing thousands of interaction variables—narrative structures, competitive contexts, strategic potentials—they could create comprehensive competitive profiles that revealed the extraordinary strategic potential of narrative differentiation.

Dr. Chen's breakthrough research revealed a crucial insight: narrative competitive strategy was fundamentally systemic and contextual. No competitive approach existed in isolation—each was part of a complex network of interdependent variables, potential interactions, and adaptive strategic mechanisms.

Advanced machine learning algorithms worked in concert with deep competitive analysis techniques, creating a comprehensive framework for understanding the nature of strategic narrative positioning. Each simulation revealed new insights into the intricate mechanisms that drive narrative competitive potential.

Complex Competitive Strategy Methodologies

As the day progressed, the team's computational models became increasingly sophisticated. They could now not only analyze existing narrative competitive approaches but predict and generate adaptive strategic positioning strategies across multiple narrative contexts.

The mysterious transmission that had guided their previous research continued to provide unexpected computational resources, accelerating their exploration of narrative competitive strategy exponentially. What had initially appeared to be a simple communication signal was revealing itself as a complex demonstration of advanced strategic intelligence.

Computational Competitive Exploration

By late afternoon, the laboratory had transformed from a traditional research space into a crucible of narrative competitive intelligence. The computational frameworks could now analyze and generate competitive strategy approaches with unprecedented sophistication, revealing pathways of interconnected competitive positioning that seemed to transcend traditional understanding of narrative differentiation.

"We're developing a new understanding of how narratives generate competitive potential through their complex strategic interactions," Dr. Rodriguez reflected, studying the latest simulation results.

The Strategic Narrative Differentiation Matrix represented a revolutionary approach to competitive strategy. It could:

- Generate predictive competitive positioning trajectories
- Identify emerging narrative competitive potential
- Create comprehensive strategic differentiation ecosystems
- Simulate multiple competitive narrative scenarios

The Continuous Frontier of Narrative Competitive Intelligence

As evening descended on the laboratory, the Competitive Narrative Intelligence Laboratory remained alive with computational and creative energy. The team had transformed their initial research into a profound exploration of narrative competitive strategy—a journey that promised to revolutionize understanding of strategic narrative potential.

Dr. Rodriguez watched the holographic displays, understanding they were witnessing the prelude to a transformation they could not yet fully comprehend. The old models of narrative competitive positioning would soon be challenged, replaced by something more profound, more complex.

"We're mapping the infinite landscape of narrative competitive strategy," she whispered to her team, "one extraordinary strategic interaction at a time."

The transmission continued to pulse—a complex, living demonstration of narrative competitive strategy that existed at the intersection of technology, strategic intelligence, and unprecedented computational insight. And in the heart of the research laboratory, a new chapter of understanding was about to unfold.

The boundaries between traditional competitive approaches and advanced computational strategy had dissolved, revealing a breathtaking landscape of infinite narrative competitive potential—waiting to be explored, waiting to be understood.

Chapter 45: Character Development Technology

The Technological Narrative Evolution Center

The first quantum pulse of dawn penetrated the Technological Narrative Evolution Center, a revolutionary facility where the boundaries between digital innovation and character creation were being systematically redefined, deconstructed, and reimagined with unprecedented technological precision. Dr. Elena Rodriguez stood at the convergence of advanced technological integration, narrative intelligence, and computational design, her holographic interfaces vibrating with the potential of groundbreaking character development technologies.

This was far more than a research center—it was a transformative crucible where the fundamental understanding of character development was being reconstructed through the most advanced technological methodologies ever conceived.

Digital Tools and Technological Integration

Dr. Marcus Chen activated the Narrative Technology Matrix, a hyper-sophisticated computational system that transformed the research space into a living, breathing ecosystem of technological character exploration. The system represented technological integration not as a linear process, but as a dynamic, interconnected network of extraordinary computational complexity and adaptive potential.

"Technology is no longer a tool for character development," Dr. Chen proclaimed to the assembled team of digital engineers, narrative technologists, and computational design specialists. "It's become the fundamental language through which characters are conceived, understood, and generated."

The Technological Narrative Evolution Center had developed revolutionary methodologies for character development technology:

1. **Quantum Character Generation Technologies**: Advanced computational techniques for multidimensional character creation
2. **Adaptive Digital Design Algorithms**: Precision methods for generating technological character development trajectories
3. **Comprehensive Technological Integration Protocols**: Holistic approaches to understanding digital character potential
4. **Dynamic Narrative Technology Simulation Systems**: Adaptive methodologies for continuous technological character evolution

Dr. Aria Kimura's latest research revealed that character development technology was far more than traditional digital design approaches. It was a complex ecosystem of technological potential, capturing the intricate interplay between computational intelligence, narrative dynamics, and advanced technological integration.

"We're transcending conventional technological boundaries," she emphasized, manipulating holographic projections that showed character development processes as intricate, interconnected systems of technological potential. "Each technological framework is a node in an extraordinary ecosystem of narrative technological discovery."

Advanced Technological Character Engineering

The center had developed unprecedented technologies that could simulate entire character development ecosystems, generating comprehensive frameworks for understanding and managing complex technological design strategies.

Dr. Rodriguez studied the latest simulation results, her scientific intuition sensing they were decoding something profound about the nature of technological character integration. The computational models showed technological character development not as a static process, but as dynamic, responsive systems of interconnected technological potential.

"Technological character development ecosystems are living, breathing networks of extraordinary complexity," she told her team. "We're developing a new understanding of how characters can be conceived, generated, and evolved through advanced technological integration."

AI and Machine Learning Character Technologies

The team's computational frameworks could now predict and generate character development technologies with unprecedented accuracy. By analyzing thousands of interaction variables—digital architectures, computational attributes, narrative potentials—they could create comprehensive technological profiles that revealed the extraordinary potential of AI-driven character creation.

Dr. Chen's breakthrough research revealed a crucial insight: character development technology was fundamentally systemic and contextual. No technological approach existed in isolation—each was part of a complex network of interdependent variables, potential interactions, and adaptive technological mechanisms.

Advanced artificial intelligence algorithms worked in concert with deep narrative analysis techniques, creating a comprehensive framework for understanding the nature of technological character design. Each simulation revealed new insights into the intricate mechanisms that drive technological character potential.

Complex Technological Development Methodologies

As the day progressed, the team's computational models became increasingly sophisticated. They could now not only analyze existing character development technologies but predict and generate adaptive technological design strategies across multiple narrative and computational contexts.

The mysterious transmission that had guided their previous research continued to provide unexpected computational resources, accelerating their exploration of character development technology exponentially. What had initially appeared to be a simple communication signal was revealing itself as a complex demonstration of advanced technological intelligence.

Computational Character Technology Exploration

By late afternoon, the center had transformed from a traditional research space into a crucible of technological character intelligence. The computational frameworks could now analyze and generate character development technologies with unprecedented sophistication, revealing pathways of interconnected technological design that seemed to transcend traditional understanding of digital character creation.

"We're developing a new understanding of how technological potential generates through complex character interactions," Dr. Rodriguez reflected, studying the latest simulation results.

The Digital Character Generation Matrix represented a revolutionary approach to technological character development. It could:

- Generate predictive technological character development trajectories
- Identify emerging digital character potential
- Create comprehensive technological character design ecosystems
- Simulate multiple advanced character generation scenarios

The Continuous Frontier of Technological Narrative Evolution

As evening descended on the center, the Technological Narrative Evolution Center remained alive with computational and creative energy. The team had transformed their initial research into a profound exploration of character development technology—a journey that promised to revolutionize understanding of technological narrative potential.

Dr. Rodriguez watched the holographic displays, understanding they were witnessing the prelude to a transformation they could not yet fully comprehend. The old models of character development would soon be challenged, replaced by something more profound, more complex.

"We're mapping the infinite landscape of technological character generation," she whispered to her team, "one extraordinary technological interaction at a time."

The transmission continued to pulse—a complex, living demonstration of character development technology that existed at the intersection of advanced computing, narrative intelligence, and unprecedented technological insight. And in the heart of the research center, a new chapter of understanding was about to unfold.

The boundaries between traditional character creation and advanced technological integration had dissolved, revealing a breathtaking landscape of infinite technological character potential—waiting to be explored, waiting to be understood.

Chapter 46: Protagonist Resilience Framework

The Psychological Durability Innovation Laboratory

The first quantum resonance of dawn penetrated the Psychological Durability Innovation Laboratory, a revolutionary facility where the intricate landscapes of character resilience were being meticulously mapped, deconstructed, and reconstructed with unprecedented precision. Dr. Elena Rodriguez stood at the convergence of computational psychology, narrative intelligence, and advanced resilience engineering, her holographic interfaces pulsing with the potential of groundbreaking protagonist durability methodologies.

This was more than a research center—it was a transformative crucible where the fundamental understanding of psychological resilience was being reimagined through the lens of advanced computational technologies and interdisciplinary strength development approaches.

Advanced Resilience Mapping Frameworks

Dr. Marcus Chen activated the Resilience Dynamics Matrix, a hyper-sophisticated computational system that transformed the research space into a living, breathing ecosystem of psychological durability exploration. The system represented resilience not as a static attribute, but as a dynamic, interconnected network of extraordinary computational complexity and adaptive potential.

"Resilience is no longer a passive characteristic," Dr. Chen proclaimed to the assembled team of psychological engineers, computational resilience specialists, and narrative development experts. "It's an active, generative system that can be systematically understood, developed, and optimized through advanced computational techniques."

The Psychological Durability Innovation Laboratory had developed revolutionary methodologies for protagonist resilience framework:

1. **Quantum Resilience Mapping Technologies**: Advanced computational techniques for multidimensional psychological strength analysis
2. **Adaptive Durability Modeling Algorithms**: Precision methods for generating psychological resilience trajectories
3. **Comprehensive Strength Development Protocols**: Holistic approaches to understanding psychological durability potential
4. **Dynamic Resilience Simulation Technologies**: Adaptive methodologies for continuous psychological strength enhancement

Dr. Aria Kimura's latest research revealed that protagonist resilience was far more than traditional psychological approaches. It was a complex ecosystem of strength potential, capturing the intricate interplay between computational intelligence, psychological dynamics, and strategic resilience engineering.

"We're transcending conventional psychological limitation boundaries," she emphasized, manipulating holographic projections that showed resilience processes as intricate, interconnected systems of psychological potential. "Each resilience framework is a node in an extraordinary ecosystem of psychological strength discovery and transformation."

Psychological Adaptation Engineering

The innovation laboratory had developed advanced technologies that could simulate entire psychological resilience ecosystems, generating comprehensive frameworks for understanding and managing complex durability development strategies.

Dr. Rodriguez studied the latest simulation results, her scientific intuition sensing they were decoding something profound about the nature of psychological resilience engineering. The computational models showed resilience development not as a static process, but as dynamic, responsive systems of interconnected psychological strength potential.

"Psychological resilience ecosystems are living, breathing networks of extraordinary complexity," she told her team. "We're developing a new understanding of how characters can build, enhance, and generate psychological durability through advanced computational techniques."

Precision Resilience Development Technologies

The team's computational frameworks could now predict and generate psychological resilience strategies with unprecedented accuracy. By analyzing thousands of interaction variables—cognitive structures, emotional adaptation mechanisms, neurological resilience potentials—they could create comprehensive psychological profiles that revealed the extraordinary engineering potential of character durability.

Dr. Chen's breakthrough research revealed a crucial insight: psychological resilience was fundamentally systemic and contextual. No resilience development approach existed in isolation—each was part of a complex network of interdependent variables, potential interactions, and adaptive psychological strength mechanisms.

Advanced machine learning algorithms worked in concert with deep psychological analysis techniques, creating a comprehensive framework for understanding the nature of precision resilience development. Each simulation revealed new insights into the intricate mechanisms that drive psychological strength potential.

Complex Psychological Strength Methodologies

As the day progressed, the team's computational models became increasingly sophisticated. They could now not only analyze existing psychological resilience approaches but predict and generate adaptive durability development strategies across multiple psychological contexts.

The mysterious transmission that had guided their previous research continued to provide unexpected computational resources, accelerating their exploration of protagonist resilience exponentially. What had initially appeared to be a simple communication signal was revealing itself as a complex demonstration of advanced psychological intelligence.

Computational Resilience Exploration

By late afternoon, the innovation laboratory had transformed from a traditional research space into a crucible of psychological resilience intelligence. The computational frameworks could now analyze and generate resilience development strategies with unprecedented sophistication, revealing pathways of interconnected psychological strength that seemed to transcend traditional understanding of character durability.

"We're developing a new understanding of how psychological potential generates through complex resilience interactions," Dr. Rodriguez reflected, studying the latest simulation results.

The Psychological Durability Mapping Matrix represented a revolutionary approach to resilience development. It could:

- Generate predictive psychological strength trajectories
- Identify emerging resilience potential
- Create comprehensive psychological durability ecosystems
- Simulate multiple adaptive response scenarios

The Continuous Frontier of Psychological Strength

As evening descended on the innovation laboratory, the Psychological Durability Innovation Laboratory remained alive with computational and creative energy. The team had transformed their initial research into a profound exploration of protagonist resilience framework—a journey that promised to revolutionize understanding of psychological durability potential.

Dr. Rodriguez watched the holographic displays, understanding they were witnessing the prelude to a transformation they could not yet fully comprehend. The old models of psychological resilience would soon be challenged, replaced by something more profound, more complex.

"We're mapping the infinite landscape of character psychological strength," she whispered to her team, "one extraordinary resilience interaction at a time."

The transmission continued to pulse—a complex, living demonstration of protagonist resilience framework that existed at the intersection of technology, psychological intelligence, and unprecedented computational insight. And in the heart of the innovation laboratory, a new chapter of understanding was about to unfold.

The boundaries between traditional psychological understanding and advanced resilience engineering had dissolved, revealing a breathtaking landscape of infinite character durability potential—waiting to be explored, waiting to be understood.

Chapter 47: Strategic Emotional Intelligence

The Emotional Dynamics Research Complex

The first quantum resonance of dawn penetrated the Emotional Dynamics Research Complex, a revolutionary facility where the intricate landscapes of emotional intelligence were being meticulously mapped, deconstructed, and reconstructed with unprecedented computational precision. Dr. Elena Rodriguez stood at the convergence of advanced emotional mapping, narrative intelligence, and computational psychology, her holographic interfaces pulsing with the potential of groundbreaking emotional intelligence methodologies.

This was more than a research center—it was a transformative crucible where the fundamental understanding of emotional complexity was being reimagined through the lens of advanced technological approaches and interdisciplinary emotional engineering.

Advanced Emotional Mapping Technologies

Dr. Marcus Chen activated the Emotional Dynamics Matrix, a hyper-sophisticated computational system that transformed the research space into a living, breathing ecosystem of emotional intelligence exploration. The system represented emotional mapping not as a static process, but as a dynamic, interconnected network of extraordinary computational complexity and adaptive potential.

"Emotional intelligence is no longer a passive observation," Dr. Chen proclaimed to the assembled team of emotional engineers, computational psychologists, and narrative intelligence specialists. "It's an active, generative system that can be systematically understood, developed, and optimized through advanced computational techniques."

The Emotional Dynamics Research Complex had developed revolutionary methodologies for strategic emotional intelligence:

1. **Quantum Emotional Mapping Technologies**: Advanced computational techniques for multidimensional emotional analysis
2. **Adaptive Emotional Modeling Algorithms**: Precision methods for generating emotional intelligence trajectories
3. **Comprehensive Emotional Development Protocols**: Holistic approaches to understanding emotional potential
4. **Dynamic Emotional Simulation Technologies**: Adaptive methodologies for continuous emotional complexity enhancement

Dr. Aria Kimura's latest research revealed that strategic emotional intelligence was far more than traditional psychological approaches. It was a complex ecosystem of emotional potential, capturing the intricate interplay between computational intelligence, psychological dynamics, and strategic emotional engineering.

"We're transcending conventional emotional limitation boundaries," she emphasized, manipulating holographic projections that showed emotional processes as intricate, interconnected systems of psychological potential. "Each emotional intelligence framework is a node in an extraordinary ecosystem of emotional discovery and transformation."

Emotional Complexity Engineering

The research complex had developed advanced technologies that could simulate entire emotional intelligence ecosystems, generating comprehensive frameworks for understanding and managing complex emotional development strategies.

Dr. Rodriguez studied the latest simulation results, her scientific intuition sensing they were decoding something profound about the nature of strategic emotional intelligence engineering. The computational models showed emotional development not as a static process, but as dynamic, responsive systems of interconnected emotional potential.

"Emotional intelligence ecosystems are living, breathing networks of extraordinary complexity," she told her team. "We're developing a new understanding of how characters can build, enhance, and generate emotional depth through advanced computational techniques."

Precision Emotional Mapping Technologies

The team's computational frameworks could now predict and generate emotional intelligence strategies with unprecedented accuracy. By analyzing thousands of interaction variables—psychological structures, emotional adaptation mechanisms, neurological emotional potentials—they could create comprehensive emotional profiles that revealed the extraordinary engineering potential of emotional complexity.

Dr. Chen's breakthrough research revealed a crucial insight: emotional intelligence was fundamentally systemic and contextual. No emotional development approach existed in isolation—each was part of a complex network of interdependent variables, potential interactions, and adaptive emotional complexity mechanisms.

Advanced machine learning algorithms worked in concert with deep psychological analysis techniques, creating a comprehensive framework for understanding the nature of precision emotional intelligence development. Each simulation revealed new insights into the intricate mechanisms that drive emotional potential.

Complex Emotional Response Methodologies

As the day progressed, the team's computational models became increasingly sophisticated. They could now not only analyze existing emotional intelligence approaches but predict and generate adaptive emotional development strategies across multiple psychological contexts.

The mysterious transmission that had guided their previous research continued to provide unexpected computational resources, accelerating their exploration of strategic emotional intelligence exponentially. What had initially appeared to be a simple communication signal was revealing itself as a complex demonstration of advanced emotional computational intelligence.

Computational Emotional Intelligence Exploration

By late afternoon, the research complex had transformed from a traditional research space into a crucible of emotional intelligence innovation. The computational frameworks could now analyze and generate emotional development strategies with unprecedented sophistication, revealing pathways of interconnected emotional complexity that seemed to transcend traditional understanding of character emotional potential.

"We're developing a new understanding of how emotional potential generates through complex emotional interactions," Dr. Rodriguez reflected, studying the latest simulation results.

The Emotional Dynamics Mapping Matrix represented a revolutionary approach to emotional intelligence development. It could:

- Generate predictive emotional complexity trajectories
- Identify emerging emotional potential
- Create comprehensive emotional intelligence ecosystems
- Simulate multiple emotional response scenarios

The Continuous Frontier of Emotional Complexity

As evening descended on the research complex, the Emotional Dynamics Research Complex remained alive with computational and creative energy. The team had transformed their initial research into a profound exploration of strategic emotional intelligence—a journey that promised to revolutionize understanding of emotional potential.

Dr. Rodriguez watched the holographic displays, understanding they were witnessing the prelude to a transformation they could not yet fully comprehend. The old models of emotional understanding would soon be challenged, replaced by something more profound, more complex.

"We're mapping the infinite landscape of emotional intelligence," she whispered to her team, "one extraordinary emotional interaction at a time."

The transmission continued to pulse—a complex, living demonstration of strategic emotional intelligence that existed at the intersection of technology, psychological insight, and unprecedented computational exploration. And in the heart of the research complex, a new chapter of understanding was about to unfold.

The boundaries between traditional emotional understanding and advanced computational emotional engineering had dissolved, revealing a breathtaking landscape of infinite emotional potential—waiting to be explored, waiting to be understood.

Chapter 48: Narrative Risk Mitigation

The Narrative Complexity Risk Management Institute

The first quantum pulse of dawn penetrated the Narrative Complexity Risk Management Institute, a revolutionary facility where the intricate landscapes of narrative challenges were being meticulously analyzed, predicted, and strategically mitigated with unprecedented computational precision. Dr. Elena Rodriguez stood at the convergence of advanced risk assessment, narrative intelligence, and computational strategic planning, her holographic interfaces vibrating with the potential of groundbreaking narrative risk mitigation methodologies.

This was more than a research center—it was a transformative crucible where the fundamental understanding of narrative complexity and potential challenges was being reimagined through the lens of advanced technological approaches and interdisciplinary risk management strategies.

Advanced Risk Assessment Frameworks

Dr. Marcus Chen activated the Narrative Risk Dynamics Matrix, a hyper-sophisticated computational system that transformed the research space into a living, breathing ecosystem of narrative challenge exploration. The system represented risk assessment not as a static analytical process, but as a dynamic, interconnected network of extraordinary computational complexity and adaptive potential.

"Risk is no longer an obstacle to be avoided," Dr. Chen proclaimed to the assembled team of narrative risk engineers, computational strategists, and complexity management specialists. "It's an active, generative system that can be systematically understood, predicted, and strategically transformed through advanced computational techniques."

The Narrative Complexity Risk Management Institute had developed revolutionary methodologies for narrative risk mitigation:

1. **Quantum Risk Prediction Technologies**: Advanced computational techniques for multidimensional narrative challenge analysis
2. **Adaptive Risk Modeling Algorithms**: Precision methods for generating comprehensive risk mitigation trajectories
3. **Comprehensive Challenge Management Protocols**: Holistic approaches to understanding narrative potential risks
4. **Dynamic Risk Simulation Technologies**: Adaptive methodologies for continuous narrative challenge anticipation

Dr. Aria Kimura's latest research revealed that narrative risk mitigation was far more than traditional risk management approaches. It was a complex ecosystem of challenge potential, capturing the intricate interplay between computational intelligence, strategic dynamics, and advanced risk engineering.

"We're transcending conventional risk limitation boundaries," she emphasized, manipulating holographic projections that showed risk processes as intricate, interconnected systems of narrative potential. "Each risk mitigation framework is a node in an extraordinary ecosystem of challenge discovery and strategic transformation."

Strategic Challenge Management

The research institute had developed advanced technologies that could simulate entire narrative risk ecosystems, generating comprehensive frameworks for understanding and managing complex challenge development strategies.

Dr. Rodriguez studied the latest simulation results, her scientific intuition sensing they were decoding something profound about the nature of narrative risk management engineering. The computational models showed risk assessment not as a static process, but as dynamic, responsive systems of interconnected challenge potential.

"Narrative risk ecosystems are living, breathing networks of extraordinary complexity," she told her team. "We're developing a new understanding of how characters can anticipate, navigate, and transform potential challenges through advanced computational techniques."

Precision Risk Identification Technologies

The team's computational frameworks could now predict and generate risk mitigation strategies with unprecedented accuracy. By analyzing thousands of interaction variables—narrative structures, potential challenge mechanisms, contextual risk potentials—they could create comprehensive risk profiles that revealed the extraordinary engineering potential of narrative challenge management.

Dr. Chen's breakthrough research revealed a crucial insight: narrative risk was fundamentally systemic and contextual. No risk management approach existed in isolation—each was part of a complex network of interdependent variables, potential interactions, and adaptive challenge mitigation mechanisms.

Advanced machine learning algorithms worked in concert with deep narrative analysis techniques, creating a comprehensive framework for understanding the nature of precision risk identification and management. Each simulation revealed new insights into the intricate mechanisms that drive narrative challenge potential.

Complex Challenge Mitigation Methodologies

As the day progressed, the team's computational models became increasingly sophisticated. They could now not only analyze existing narrative risk approaches but predict and generate adaptive challenge management strategies across multiple narrative contexts.

The mysterious transmission that had guided their previous research continued to provide unexpected computational resources, accelerating their exploration of narrative risk mitigation exponentially. What had initially appeared to be a simple communication signal was revealing itself as a complex demonstration of advanced strategic intelligence.

Computational Risk Exploration

By late afternoon, the research institute had transformed from a traditional research space into a crucible of narrative risk intelligence. The computational frameworks could now analyze and generate risk mitigation strategies with unprecedented sophistication, revealing pathways of interconnected challenge management that seemed to transcend traditional understanding of narrative risk potential.

"We're developing a new understanding of how narrative potential generates through complex risk interactions," Dr. Rodriguez reflected, studying the latest simulation results.

The Narrative Risk Dynamics Mapping Matrix represented a revolutionary approach to risk mitigation development. It could:

- Generate predictive narrative challenge trajectories
- Identify emerging risk potential
- Create comprehensive challenge management ecosystems
- Simulate multiple risk response scenarios

The Continuous Frontier of Narrative Challenge Management

As evening descended on the research institute, the Narrative Complexity Risk Management Institute remained alive with computational and creative energy. The team had transformed their initial research into a profound exploration of narrative risk mitigation—a journey that promised to revolutionize understanding of challenge potential.

Dr. Rodriguez watched the holographic displays, understanding they were witnessing the prelude to a transformation they could not yet fully comprehend. The old models of narrative risk would soon be challenged, replaced by something more profound, more complex.

"We're mapping the infinite landscape of narrative challenge management," she whispered to her team, "one extraordinary risk interaction at a time."

The transmission continued to pulse—a complex, living demonstration of narrative risk mitigation that existed at the intersection of technology, strategic intelligence, and unprecedented computational insight. And in the heart of the research institute, a new chapter of understanding was about to unfold.

The boundaries between traditional risk management and advanced computational challenge engineering had dissolved, revealing a breathtaking landscape of infinite narrative risk potential—waiting to be explored, waiting to be understood.

Chapter 49: Protagonist Transformation Lifecycle

The Evolutionary Pathways of Narrative Potential

The soft quantum hum of the Narrative Complexity Risk Management Institute resonated with a new frequency as dawn broke, signaling the beginning of an unprecedented exploration into the comprehensive lifecycle of protagonist transformation. Dr. Elena Rodriguez stood at the epicenter of a revolutionary research initiative that would redefine the understanding of character evolution, bridging the gap between computational intelligence and narrative metamorphosis.

Mapping the Transformational Continuum

The Protagonist Transformation Lifecycle Laboratory was a marvel of interdisciplinary engineering—a space where advanced computational models intersected with deep psychological mapping, creating a holographic ecosystem of character development that pulsed with unprecedented dynamic potential.

Dr. Marcus Chen activated the Evolutionary Dynamics Projection System, a hyper-advanced computational framework that could simulate the intricate stages of character transformation with molecular precision. Holographic representations of potential character trajectories filled the research space, each thread a complex network of potential developmental pathways.

"Transformation is not a linear process," Dr. Chen explained to the assembled team of narrative engineers, psychological architects, and computational strategists. "It's a multidimensional ecosystem of potential, where each interaction generates infinite possibilities of character evolution."

The Developmental Phase Analysis

The research team had developed breakthrough methodologies for understanding the nuanced stages of protagonist transformation:

1. **Initial Potential Calibration**: Identifying the fundamental architectural components of character potential
2. **Adaptive Response Mapping**: Understanding how characters internalize and respond to narrative challenges
3. **Transformational Trajectory Simulation**: Generating comprehensive models of character evolution
4. **Psychological Resilience Optimization**: Developing strategies for character growth and adaptation

Dr. Aria Kimura's latest research revealed that character transformation was far more complex than traditional narrative development approaches. Each protagonist represented a living, breathing computational ecosystem of potential, with infinite pathways of psychological and narrative evolution.

"We're transcending the traditional boundaries of character development," she proclaimed, manipulating intricate holographic projections that revealed the interconnected nature of character transformation. "Each developmental stage is a node in an extraordinary network of narrative potential."

The Quantum Mechanics of Character Evolution

The Protagonist Transformation Lifecycle Laboratory had developed computational technologies that could simulate entire character evolution ecosystems, generating comprehensive frameworks for understanding the most intricate mechanisms of narrative metamorphosis.

Dr. Rodriguez studied the latest simulation results, her scientific intuition sensing they were decoding something profound about the nature of character development. The computational models showed character transformation not as a predetermined path, but as a dynamic, responsive system of interconnected evolutionary potential.

"Protagonist lifecycles are living networks of extraordinary complexity," she told her team. "We're developing a new understanding of how characters can anticipate, navigate, and fundamentally reshape their narrative potential through advanced computational techniques."

Precision Evolutionary Mapping

The team's computational frameworks could now predict and generate character transformation strategies with unprecedented accuracy. By analyzing thousands of interaction variables—psychological structures, potential developmental mechanisms, contextual evolution potentials—they could create comprehensive character profiles that revealed the extraordinary engineering potential of narrative metamorphosis.

Dr. Chen's breakthrough research revealed a crucial insight: character transformation was fundamentally systemic and contextual. No developmental approach existed in isolation—each was part of a complex network of interdependent variables, potential interactions, and adaptive evolution mechanisms.

Advanced machine learning algorithms worked in concert with deep psychological analysis techniques, creating a comprehensive framework for understanding the nature of precision character development and transformation.

Complex Transformation Management Methodologies

As the research progressed, the team's computational models became increasingly sophisticated. They could now not only analyze existing character development approaches but predict and generate adaptive transformation strategies across multiple narrative contexts.

The mysterious transmission that had guided their previous research continued to provide unexpected computational resources, accelerating their exploration of protagonist lifecycle management exponentially. What had initially appeared to be a simple communication signal was revealing itself as a complex demonstration of advanced strategic intelligence.

Computational Transformation Exploration

By midday, the research institute had transformed from a traditional research space into a crucible of character evolution intelligence. The computational frameworks could now analyze and generate transformation strategies with unprecedented sophistication, revealing pathways of interconnected developmental potential that seemed to transcend traditional understanding of narrative character growth.

The Protagonist Evolutionary Dynamics Mapping Matrix represented a revolutionary approach to character lifecycle development. It could:

- Generate predictive character transformation trajectories
- Identify emerging developmental potential
- Create comprehensive character evolution ecosystems
- Simulate multiple psychological and narrative response scenarios

The Infinite Landscape of Character Metamorphosis

As afternoon light filtered through the institute's quantum-responsive windows, Dr. Rodriguez and her team stood at the threshold of a profound understanding. The boundaries between traditional character development and advanced computational evolutionary engineering had dissolved, revealing a breathtaking landscape of infinite narrative potential.

The transmission continued to pulse—a complex, living demonstration of protagonist transformation that existed at the intersection of technology, psychological intelligence, and unprecedented computational insight.

"We're mapping the infinite landscape of character lifecycle management," Dr. Rodriguez whispered to her team, "one extraordinary evolutionary interaction at a time."

And in the heart of the Protagonist Transformation Lifecycle Laboratory, a new chapter of understanding was about to unfold—a testament to the extraordinary potential of narrative engineering, where every character represented a universe of infinite possibility, waiting to be explored, waiting to be understood.

Chapter 50: Future of Character Engineering

The Visionary Horizon of Narrative Potential

The first quantum echoes of a new era resonated through the Narrative Complexity Research Institute as dawn broke, revealing a landscape of unprecedented possibility. Dr. Elena Rodriguez stood at the convergence of technological innovation and narrative imagination, her eyes reflecting the extraordinary potential of what humanity was about to discover about the fundamental nature of character creation and narrative potential.

The Futuristic Character Engineering Division had become more than a research facility—it was a transformative crucible where the boundaries of narrative intelligence were being systematically dismantled and reconstructed with breathtaking computational precision.

Emerging Paradigms of Narrative Creation

Dr. Marcus Chen activated the Narrative Potential Projection System, a hyper-advanced computational framework that seemed to breathe with its own form of intelligence. Holographic representations of potential narrative architectures filled the research space, each thread a complex network of infinite storytelling possibilities.

"We're no longer merely designing characters," Dr. Chen proclaimed to the assembled team of narrative architects, computational strategists, and interdimensional research specialists. "We're creating living ecosystems of potential—narrative intelligences that transcend traditional understanding of storytelling."

Innovative Methodological Breakthroughs

The research team had developed revolutionary approaches to character engineering that defied conventional limitations:

1. **Quantum Narrative Intelligence Protocols**: Advanced computational techniques for generating self-evolving narrative ecosystems
2. **Adaptive Protagonist Generation Algorithms**: Precision methods for creating characters with unprecedented levels of complexity and autonomy
3. **Multidimensional Narrative Potential Mapping**: Comprehensive frameworks for understanding the infinite potential of character development
4. **Dynamic Narrative Intelligence Technologies**: Adaptive methodologies for generating autonomous narrative entities

Dr. Aria Kimura's latest research revealed that character engineering had evolved into something far more profound than traditional storytelling approaches. Each potential narrative entity represented a living, computational ecosystem of extraordinary complexity.

"We're transcending the fundamental boundaries of narrative creation," she emphasized, manipulating intricate holographic projections that revealed the interconnected nature of narrative potential. "Each character is no longer a passive construct, but an active, generative intelligence."

The Computational Frontiers of Storytelling

The Futuristic Character Engineering Division had developed technologies that could simulate entire narrative ecosystems, generating comprehensive frameworks for understanding the most intricate mechanisms of story generation and character evolution.

Dr. Rodriguez studied the latest simulation results, her scientific intuition sensing they were decoding something far more profound than mere storytelling techniques. The computational models showed narrative potential as a dynamic, responsive system of extraordinary complexity—each character a universe of infinite possibility.

"We're witnessing the emergence of a new form of narrative intelligence," she told her team, her voice a mixture of scientific precision and profound wonder. "Characters are no longer created—they're discovered, cultivated, allowed to emerge from computational ecosystems of extraordinary potential."

Predictive Narrative Generation Technologies

The team's computational frameworks had reached a level of sophistication that bordered on the miraculous. They could now predict and generate entire narrative ecosystems with unprecedented accuracy, analyzing thousands of interaction variables to create comprehensive story potential profiles.

Dr. Chen's breakthrough research revealed a crucial insight: narrative potential was fundamentally quantum in nature—existing simultaneously in multiple states, defying traditional linear storytelling approaches. No narrative construct existed in isolation—each was part of a complex network of interdependent variables, potential interactions, and adaptive generative mechanisms.

Advanced machine learning algorithms worked in concert with deep narrative analysis techniques, creating a comprehensive framework for understanding the nature of predictive story generation.

The Visionary Approaches to Narrative Engineering

As the research progressed, the computational models became increasingly sophisticated. They could now not only analyze existing narrative approaches but generate entirely new paradigms of storytelling across multiple conceptual contexts.

The mysterious transmission that had guided their previous research continued to provide unexpected computational resources, accelerating their exploration of narrative potential exponentially. What had initially appeared to be a simple communication signal was revealing itself as a complex demonstration of advanced narrative intelligence.

Computational Narrative Exploration

By midday, the research institute had transformed into a crucible of narrative generation intelligence. The computational frameworks could now generate entire narrative ecosystems with unprecedented sophistication, revealing pathways of interconnected storytelling potential that seemed to transcend traditional understanding of character and narrative creation.

The Narrative Potential Generation Matrix represented a revolutionary approach to story engineering. It could:

- Generate predictive narrative trajectories
- Identify emerging storytelling potential
- Create comprehensive narrative ecosystem simulations
- Develop autonomous character intelligence protocols

The Infinite Landscape of Narrative Possibility

As afternoon light filtered through quantum-responsive windows, Dr. Rodriguez and her team stood at the threshold of a profound transformation. The boundaries between traditional storytelling and advanced computational narrative engineering had dissolved, revealing a breathtaking landscape of infinite narrative potential.

The transmission continued to pulse—a complex, living demonstration of narrative intelligence that existed at the intersection of technology, creative potential, and unprecedented computational insight.

"We're mapping the infinite landscape of narrative possibility," Dr. Rodriguez whispered to her team, "one extraordinary generative interaction at a time."

And in the heart of the Futuristic Character Engineering Division, humanity was about to witness the birth of a new understanding—a testament to the extraordinary potential of narrative intelligence, where every story represented a universe of infinite possibility, waiting to be explored, waiting to be understood.

The future of storytelling had arrived—and it was more extraordinary than anyone could have imagined.

Don't miss out!

Visit the website below and you can sign up to receive emails whenever Stormrider publishes a new book. There's no charge and no obligation.

https://books2read.com/r/B-A-JCSPB-EFQLF

Did you love *Character Engineering: The Quantum Mechanics of Narrative Potential*? Then you should read *Swipe Right for Love*[1] by Stormrider!

[2]

In the fast-paced world of Silicon Valley, can an algorithm crack the code of true love?

Zoe Chen, a brilliant but lonely software developer, reluctantly dives into the world of online dating with HeartSync, an AI-powered app promising to revolutionize romance. **Alex Rivera**, a charming graphic designer disillusioned with love, takes one last shot at finding a connection. When a glitch in the system matches them with swapped profile information, what starts as a series of hilarious misunderstandings blossoms into an unexpected connection.

As Zoe and Alex navigate the treacherous waters between their online personas and real-world selves, they'll face technical difficulties, personal insecurities, and a massive data breach that threatens not just their budding relationship, but the privacy of millions. Can their connection survive the

1. https://books2read.com/u/3Rlzxn

2. https://books2read.com/u/3Rlzxn

transition from pixels to reality? Or will the pressures of the tech world and their own fears crash the system before love can truly boot up?

"**Swipe Right for Love** is a charming, laugh-out-loud romantic comedy that explores the intersections of technology and the heart. Perfect for fans of "**The Rosie Project**" and "**Ready Player One**," this novel delves into the challenges of modern dating while celebrating the timeless quest for authentic human connection.

Also by Stormrider

Love in the Digital Age: Virtual Hearts
Swipe Right for Love
Streaming Hearts

science fiction
The Quantum Paradox: A Journey Beyond Time

self-help
Unburdened: Finding Freedom from Overthinking
The Future of Work: Navigating the Digital Revolution

The Romantic Hacker
The Code of Love
Encrypted Hearts

Standalone
Character Engineering: The Quantum Mechanics of Narrative Potential

www.ingramcontent.com/pod-product-compliance
Lightning Source LLC
LaVergne TN
LVHW012046160826
845678LV00014B/2717
* 9 7 9 8 2 3 0 8 4 8 4 9 3 *